The Queen's Faith

Queen Elizabeth II
Describes Her Faith

Edited by Geoffrey Waugh

The Queen's Faith

Queen Elizabeth II
Describes the Significance of her Christian Faith
2021

Also available in Basic and Gift Editions and eBooks as published by Renewal Journal Publications – www.renewaljournal.com

Cover Design: Jay Cookingham

See also
The Queen's Christmas & Easter Messages: Queen Elizabeth II describes the Significance of Christmas & Easter.

The Queen's Christmas & Easter Messages has a double page for each year of The Queen's reign and includes excerpts also included in this book where they are arranged here in themes.

Cover photo: Her Majesty Queen Elizabeth II, in the first colour television broadcast of her Christmas Message, 1967.

The Royal Family: Christmas Broadcasts, 1952-2020. Excerpts.

Sources are acknowledged, and will be, where known. Images are from common domain sites including photographs from *The Telegraph* of London.

ISBN: 978-1-60383-602-9

Holy Fire Publishing
5016 Spedale Ct., Spring Hill, TN 37174
www.holyfirepublishing.com

Gift Edition: ISBN 9798501268067 (in colour)

www.renewaljournal.com

Renewal Journal

♛

A tribute to

Her Majesty

Queen Elizabeth II

with appreciation

Contents

A Blog for this book is on
www.renewaljournal.com

The Queen's Faith

Queen Elizabeth II
describes her faith
in Her Majesty's own words
with excerpts drawn primarily from her
annual Christmas broadcasts.

Christians of all races, nations and
denominations believe the immortal
words of John's Gospel:

For God so loved the world that He gave
His only begotten Son, that whoever
believes in Him should not perish but
have everlasting life.
(John 3:16)

Historic Easter Message

Excerpt from The Queen's historic Easter message on Easter Saturday, 2020, when churches were closed due to the Coronavirus.

Many religions have festivals which celebrate light overcoming darkness. Such occasions are often accompanied by the lighting of candles. They seem to speak to every culture, and appeal to people of all faiths, and of none. They are lit on birthday cakes and to mark family anniversaries, when we gather happily around a source of light. It unites us.

As darkness falls on the Saturday before Easter Day, many Christians would normally light candles together. In church, one light would pass to another, spreading slowly and then more rapidly as more candles are lit. It's a way of showing how the good news of Christ's resurrection has been passed on from the first Easter by every generation until now. ...

The discovery of the risen Christ on the first Easter Day gave his followers new hope and fresh purpose, and we can all take heart from this. We know that Coronavirus will not overcome us. As dark as death can be – particularly for those suffering with grief – light and life are greater.

May the living flame of the Easter hope be a steady guide as we face the future.

I wish everyone of all faiths and denominations a blessed Easter.

Quotes from The Queen's Christmas and Easter Messages

God sent into the world a unique person - neither a philosopher nor a general, important though they are, but a Saviour, with the power to forgive. Forgiveness lies at the heart of the Christian faith. (2011)

This is the time of year when we remember that God sent his only son 'to serve, not to be served'. He restored love and service to the centre of our lives in the person of Jesus Christ. (2012)

For Christians, as for all people of faith, reflection, meditation and prayer help us to renew ourselves in God's love, as we strive daily to become better people. The Christmas message shows us that this love is for everyone. There is no one beyond its reach. (2013)

For me, the life of Jesus Christ, the Prince of Peace, whose birth we celebrate today, is an inspiration and an anchor in my life. (2014)

Despite being displaced and persecuted throughout his short life, Christ's unchanging message was not one of revenge or violence but simply that we should love one another. (2015)

Jesus Christ lived obscurely for most of his life, and never travelled far. He was maligned and rejected by many, though he had done no wrong. And yet, billions of people now follow his teaching and find in him the guiding light for their lives. I am one of them because Christ's example helps me see the value of doing small things with great love, whoever does them and whatever they themselves believe. (2016)

We remember the birth of Jesus Christ, whose only sanctuary was a stable in Bethlehem. He knew rejection, hardship and persecution. And, yet, it is Jesus Christ's generous love and example which has inspired me through good times and bad. **(2017)**

The Christmas story retains its appeal since it doesn't provide theoretical explanations for the puzzles of life. Instead, it's about the birth of a child, and the hope that birth 2,000 years ago brought to the world. Only a few people acknowledged Jesus when he was born; now billions follow him. I believe his message of peace on earth and goodwill to all is never out of date. It can be heeded by everyone. It's needed as much as ever. **(2018)**

Of course, at the heart of the Christmas story lies the birth of a child, a seemingly small and insignificant step overlooked by many in Bethlehem. But in time, through his teaching and by his example, Jesus Christ would show the world how small steps, taken in faith and in hope, can overcome long-held differences and deep-seated divisions to bring harmony and understanding. **(2019)**

The discovery of the risen Christ on the first Easter Day gave his followers new hope and fresh purpose, and we can all take heart from this. … May the living flame of the Easter hope be a steady guide as we face the future. **(2020)**

The Queen's quotations are printed in **bold italic** in this book.

The Queen's Faith

Queen Elizabeth II
describes her Faith

"Peace on earth, Goodwill toward all" ~
the eternal message of Christmas,
and the desire of us all

The Queen has spoken about the significance of Christmas to more people than anyone else in history

Her Majesty's historic Easter Message in 2020 was broadcast when churches were closed due to the coronavirus pandemic

These Messages point to
light in the darkness
life amidst death
faith dispelling fear
hope for the hopeless
love overcoming all

Introduction

Prince Philip, the Duke of Edinburgh (10 June 1921 – 9 April 2021) who died two months before his 100th birthday, the longest serving royal consort in British history, encouraged The Queen to talk about her Christian faith in her Christmas broadcast of 2000, celebrating the second millennium since the birth of Jesus Christ.

Rev Prof Ian Bradley, the author of *God Save the Queen*, spoke to Premier Christian News about his memories of the Duke:

He was the person really who encouraged the queen to talk about her own faith in her Christmas broadcasts. You know, in the old days, they really used to be more like travelogues, and they would just say where the royal family had been.

But in 2000, the Queen's spoke very movingly and powerfully about her own Christian faith and the impact it had on her. And there was a very positive response from viewers. And Philip, it was Philip who really persuaded the queen to make more of her own Christian faith and he said, 'You should be talking about this.'

Rev Prof Ian Bradley preached for the Queen and for the Duke of Edinburgh as a visiting preacher at the Parish of Braemar and Crathie where The Queen visits the church for Sunday services when staying at Balmoral. He said that Prince Philip liked to take notes during sermons and he was extremely interested in theology:

He would note down all the details of the sermon. He was extremely interested in, in theology, he had a wonderful knowledge of the Bible, and then he would sort of quiz you at lunchtime, ask you about your sermon and really put you on your mettle. And I was amazed at his biblical knowledge. I mean, we sat up one evening, talking almost far into the night about biblical references to the environment, his great interest, of course. He was he was very well steeped in the Bible, but he was particularly interested in what the Bible had to say about creation and our relationship with creation.

From Premier Christian News article by Chantalle Edmunds, Saturday 10 April 2021.

[https://premierchristian.news/en/news/article/prince-philip-persuaded-the-queen-to-talk-for-the-first-time-about-her-own-faith-in-christmas-broadcast.]

An article in The Guardian by Catherine Pepinster, published on Sunday 24 December 2017, described how The Queen has spoken about her Christian faith.

[https://www.theguardian.com/uk-ews/2017/dec/24/queens-christmas-message-article-of-christian-faith]

To the royal household, it is known as the QXB – the Queen's Christmas broadcast. To millions of people, it is still an essential feature of Christmas Day. To the Queen, her annual broadcast is the time when she speaks to the nation without the government scripting it. But in recent years, it has also become something else: a declaration of her Christian faith. As Britain has become more secular, the Queen's messages have followed the opposite trajectory.

A survey of the broadcasts made during her 65-year reign reveals that for most of the time the Queen has spoken only in passing of the religious significance of Christmas. ...

But for the past 17 years, her messages have taken on a different tone, with the Queen explaining her own personal faith – "the anchor in my life", as she described it in 2014.

Last year she said: "Billions of people now follow Christ's teaching and find in him the guiding light for their lives. I am one of them because Christ's example helps me see the value of doing small things with great love, whoever does them and whatever they themselves believe."

The turning point in the content of the broadcasts was the millennium. Her broadcast in 2000 was devoted to an account of Christ's life and teaching which, she said, "provide a framework in which I try to lead my life".

This personal commentary has continued ever since. According to Ian Bradley, professor of cultural and spiritual history at the University of St Andrews and the author of *God Save the Queen – The Spiritual Heart of the Monarchy*, "this truly makes her Defender of the Faith" – a reference to the title that all monarchs have used since it was first bestowed on Henry VIII in 1521 by Pope Leo X before he broke with Rome. Indeed, Elizabeth II's faith impresses the papacy today, so much that one senior Vatican official described her to me as "the last Christian monarch".

Explanations for these overtly Christian messages vary. Some royal watchers suggest that it was the Queen's decision to use the 2,000th anniversary of Christ's birth as an opportunity to speak openly about Christianity. Others saw the hand of George Carey, then archbishop of Canterbury. Bradley sees the influence of Prince Philip at work. "After her very personal account in 2000, she was encouraged to continue because I'm told she received 25 times more letters than usual from the public in response to that Christmas message than others, and she had huge support from the Duke of Edinburgh."

But Stephen Bates, a former royal correspondent and author of *Royalty Inc: Britain's Best-Known Brand*, believes it was the death of the Queen Mother that changed her. "She loosened up after her mother's death. The Queen Mother kept a beady eye on her and now she is more relaxed," he said. "She expresses more of what she feels. I think this openness about her own commitment is part of it as well."

Before 2000, the Queen's most explicit commitments of faith were made during a 1947 radio broadcast, when she spoke of dedicating her life to service, and ended it by saying, "God help me to make good my vow" and at her coronation service.

Accession to the throne also meant she became supreme governor of the Church of England, the established church, and since then her public life has been inextricably shaped by religious occasions: being seen by TV audiences at church at Christmas and Easter, distributing Maundy money on Maundy Thursday and attending the Remembrance Sunday service at the Cenotaph.

But it is the Christmas broadcast where the personal, as well as public, is evident. No government official is involved. Instead, those who cast an eye in advance over what she has written will be her private secretary, now Edward Young, as well as the Duke of Edinburgh. Lord Chartres, the recently retired bishop of London, has long been the go-to theological adviser to the royal family and is believed to proffer advice as well. Regular themes include forgiveness, reconciliation, compassion and, most often, service.

Lord Williams of Oystermouth, who, as Dr Rowan Williams, served as archbishop of Canterbury from 2002 to 2012, said that at times Lambeth Palace was consulted. "We were occasionally asked for any thoughts we might want to throw in."

Last week, the BBC admitted that it has been reflecting a secular version of Britain and needs to do more to hold up a mirror to faith in Britain. According to Williams, the Queen has been bridging the divide. "I think that as there has been less overt Christian 'messaging' in the general cultural

14

environment, the Queen has deliberately decided to fill the gap," he said.

The recent messages always refer to Britons of other faiths, too. Williams also sees a link between the recent Christmas messages and a landmark speech the Queen made in 2012 at Lambeth Palace at the start of her diamond jubilee year, when she described the Church of England as, in effect, an umbrella under which other faiths could shelter.

"I think it is related to her position as supreme governor and in line with her speech at Lambeth in 2012 about the Church of England's responsibility to be a positive gatekeeper for faith at large in the nation, without sacrificing its particularity," he said.

The tradition of the royal Christmas message was begun in 1932 by the Queen's grandfather, George V, and continued under her father, George VI. "George V wasn't particularly devout but the Queen's father was," said Bradley. They began as radio broadcasts but became televised in 1957 and have been recorded at Buckingham Palace – once, famously, by David Attenborough in 1986 in a stable at the Royal Mews – Windsor Castle and Sandringham in Norfolk.

This book shows how Her Majesty The Queen has often spoken about her faith including during the years before 2000.

This book draws on the Queen's Christmas broadcasts throughout her long reign, as well as her Easter broadcast in 2020. Many of Her Majesty's statements about the Christian faith are compiled into the most commonly expressed themes about Jesus Christ, faith, love, compassion, forgiveness, reconciliation and service.

Consequently, these statements of faith are primarily given in the context of the celebration of Christmas, that annual global festival commemorating the birth of Jesus Christ.

15

Here I reproduce some of the first accounts of that momentous event, the birth of a baby in Bethlehem, a small village 8 miles south of the old city of Jerusalem. The year in our calendars and diaries are a reminder of the approximate number of years which have passed since that historic birth.

I reproduce these excerpts from each of the Queen's annual Christmas broadcasts in my companion book *The Queen's Christmas & Easter Messages*.

The Christmas and Easter Messages, first told and written 2000 years ago, are now celebrated around the world. Christmas and Easter are public holidays in many countries.

Millions of people attend churches at Christmas and Easter to hear and sing the Christmas and Easter Messages. Popular readings at Christmas from the ancient stories about the unique baby's birth were first written on parchment in the Gospels of Luke and Matthew.

The translators of the New Revised Standard Version of the Bible, first published in 1989, acknowledged the majesty of the King James Version in their introductory word "to the reader":

> In the course of time the King James Version came to be regarded as "the Authorized Version." With good reason it has been termed "the noblest monument of English prose," and it has entered, as no other book has, into the making of the personal character of the public institutions of the English-speaking peoples. We owe to it an incalculable debt.

Many people now prefer the New King James Version (NKJV). Those who prefer more current or modern language may like to meditate on the translation of these timeless stories in the New Revised Standard Version (NRSV), now read in many churches and used for personal study and enjoyment. The NRSV uses inclusive language, as does the original Hebrew and Greek, and includes useful section headings. Where the passage under a section heading is repeated, or has a similar passage elsewhere in the Bible, the NRSV heading gives the other references. Headings for unique passages, not repeated elsewhere, have no references, as in these unique Christmas stories in Luke and Matthew.

The Birth of Jesus

In those days a decree went out from Emperor Augustus that all the world should be registered. [2] This was the first registration and was taken while Quirinius was governor of Syria. [3] All went to their own towns to be registered. [4] Joseph also went from the town of Nazareth in Galilee to Judea, to the city of David called Bethlehem, because he was descended from the house and family of David. [5] He went to be registered with Mary, to whom he was engaged and who was expecting a child. [6] While they were there, the time came for her to deliver her child. [7] And she gave birth to her firstborn son and wrapped him in bands of cloth, and laid him in a manger, because there was no place for them in the inn.

The Shepherds and the Angels

[8] In that region there were shepherds living in the fields, keeping watch over their flock by night. [9] Then an angel of the Lord stood before them, and the glory of the Lord shone around them, and they were terrified. [10] But the angel said to them, 'Do not be afraid; for see—I am bringing you good news of great joy for all the people: [11] to you is born this day in the city of David a Saviour, who is the Messiah, the Lord. [12] This will be a sign for you: you will find a child wrapped in bands of cloth and lying in a manger.' [13] And

suddenly there was with the angel a multitude of the heavenly host, praising God and saying,

14 'Glory to God in the highest heaven,
  and on earth peace among those whom he favours!'
(Luke 2:1-14 NRSV)

The Visit of the Wise Men

In the time of King Herod, after Jesus was born in Bethlehem of Judea, wise men from the East came to Jerusalem, 2 asking, 'Where is the child who has been born king of the Jews? For we observed his star at its rising, and have come to pay him homage.' 3 When King Herod heard this, he was frightened, and all Jerusalem with him; 4 and calling together all the chief priests and scribes of the people, he inquired of them where the Messiah was to be born. 5 They told him, 'In Bethlehem of Judea; for so it has been written by the prophet:

6 "And you, Bethlehem, in the land of Judah,
  are by no means least among the rulers of Judah;
for from you shall come a ruler
  who is to shepherd my people Israel."'
7 Then Herod secretly called for the wise men and learned from them the exact time when the star had appeared. 8 Then he sent them to Bethlehem, saying, 'Go and search diligently for the child; and when you have found him, bring me word so that I may also go and pay him homage.' 9 When they had heard the king, they set out; and there, ahead of them, went the star that they had seen at its rising, until it stopped over the place where the child was. 10 When they saw that the star had stopped, they were

overwhelmed with joy. **11** On entering the house, they saw the child with Mary his mother; and they knelt down and paid him homage. Then, opening their treasure-chests, they offered him gifts of gold, frankincense, and myrrh. **12** And having been warned in a dream not to return to Herod, they left for their own country by another road.

The Escape to Egypt

13 Now after they had left, an angel of the Lord appeared to Joseph in a dream and said, 'Get up, take the child and his mother, and flee to Egypt, and remain there until I tell you; for Herod is about to search for the child, to destroy him.' **14** Then Joseph got up, took the child and his mother by night, and went to Egypt, **15** and remained there until the death of Herod. This was to fulfil what had been spoken by the Lord through the prophet, 'Out of Egypt I have called my son.'

(Matthew 2:1-15 NRSV)

These Christmas stories are Gospel readings used in church lectionaries in the Advent and Christmas seasons in December each year. Millions of people enjoy celebrating Christmas Day in church services where these and similar readings are used. It is also a time when millions enjoy singing Christmas Carols, such as those included in the Appendix of this book, in Carols by Candlelight and at other concerts. Many Carols tell these Christmas stories in beautiful, poetic lyrics.

Another valued Christmas tradition for millions of us has been listening to the Royal Christmas Message which is broadcast around the world on Christmas Day.

The Queen's first Christmas Message (1952), broadcast to millions of listeners, reminded us that "Peace on earth, Goodwill toward men" is the eternal message of Christmas, and the desire of us all.

The formal name of her Christmas Broadcast is 'Her Majesty's Most Gracious Speech.'

King George V, The Queen's grandfather, gave the first Royal Christmas Message in 1932. King George VI commenced the custom of an annual Royal Christmas Message in 1939 at the outbreak of the Second World War (1939-1945), just 21 years after the end of the First World War (1914-1918). King George VI ended his first Christmas broadcast with encouragement from the poem by Minnie Louise Haskins titled *God Knows*:

> *I said to the man who stood at the Gate of the Year, "Give me a light that I may tread safely into the unknown." And he replied, "Go out into the darkness, and put your hand into the Hand of God. That shall be to you better than light, and safer than a known way."*

The poem continues:

> So I went forth, and finding the Hand of God, trod gladly into the night.
> And He led me towards the hills and the breaking of day in the lone East.
>
> *So heart be still:*
> *What need our little life*
> *Our human life to know,*
> *If God hath comprehension?*
> *In all the dizzy strife*
> *Of things both high and low,*
> *God hideth His intention.*
>
> *God knows. His will*
> *Is best. The stretch of years*
> *Which wind ahead, so dim*
> *To our imperfect vision,*

Are clear to God. Our fears
Are premature; In Him,
All time hath full provision.

Then rest: until
God moves to lift the veil
From our impatient eyes,
When, as the sweeter features
Of Life's stern face we hail,
Fair beyond all surmise
God's thought around His creatures
Our mind shall fill.[1]

The King's quotation of "The Gate of the Year" brought it to public attention and it became an inspiration to millions throughout the world. Widely reproduced and quoted, including on the following Sunday, New Year's Eve, December 31, 1939, the poem has continued to comfort and inspire many generations.

The book **The Servant Queen and the King She Serves**, published for Queen Elizabeth II's 90th birthday, with a Foreword by the Queen, tells how the young Princess Elizabeth, aged 13, handed the poem to her father. Queen Elizabeth The Queen Mother had its words engraved on plaques on the gates of the King George VI Memorial Chapel at Windsor Castle, where the King was interred in 1952, as she was in 2002, having lived to 101.

The annual Queen's Christmas Broadcasts continue to inspire a worldwide audience. For millions, as for our family, it has been an eagerly anticipated part of Christmas Day, often following celebrations including the joyful carols of the morning church service, sharing family gifts, and enjoying the Christmas family lunch or dinner together. Our family, in Australia's summer, would sprawl around the floor and lounge chairs to relax and

---

[1] *God Knows,* privately published by the author in the collection, *The Desert,* 1912.

listen to the broadcast of the Royal Christmas Message on radio and, later on, on television. This was a welcome break amid the family's festive games such as trying out new toys or sports gear. The next day, on the Boxing Day holiday, we were back watching English and Australian cricketers compete in The Ashes series.

As technology developed, The Queen's Christmas Broadcast came to us with increasing and impressive sophistication. The early years of the crackling wireless from 1952 gave way to the magic of sight with black and white television from 1957, then to the splendours of colour TV from 1967. From 1959 the pre-recorded broadcasts gave increasing opportunity for relevant film footage to be interspersed with The Queen speaking. Millions appreciate her compassionate observations about events of the past year and about the significance of Christmas.

Jon Kuhrt wrote a blog about The Queen's Christmas messages. He was impressed by comments in the 2014 broadcast while he worked with people affected by homelessness, offending and addictions at the West London Mission. Jon wrote: "I have not been a committed viewer (apart from when I am at my Mum's when it is compulsory viewing). So I went back and read her previous Christmas messages over the last 5 years."

Here, I have adapted Jon's Resistance and Renewal blog in which he described how The Queen's Christmas messages are a model of how to talk about faith in the public sphere.

1) The Queen speaks personally
"It is my prayer this Christmas Day that Jesus' example and teaching will continue to bring people together to give the best of themselves in the service of others." (2012)
"For me, the life of Jesus Christ, the prince of peace, whose birth we celebrate today, is an inspiration and an anchor in my life." (2014)

Personal testimony is significant and convincing, causing respect in those listening. The Queen is *personal* in the way she speaks, using words like 'for me'; 'my life' and 'my prayer'.

2) The Queens speaks compassionately

"Despite being displaced and persecuted throughout his short life, Christ's unchanging message was not one of revenge or violence but simply that we should love one another." (2015)
"Christ's example helps me see the value of doing small things with great love, whoever does them and whatever they themselves believe." (2016)

Consistently, The Queen and the Royal Family show deep concern for the bereaved and suffering, both in personal contact and in correspondence. The heart of Christmas is about God's love for everyone, especially the hurting and fallen.

3) The Queen speaks inclusively

"The Christmas message shows us that this love is for everyone. There is no one beyond its reach." (2013)
"Christ's example has taught me to seek to respect and value all people, of whatever faith or none." (2014)

God's love is for *all people* and believing in this love leads us to respect and value everyone. Jon adds, "It resonated with my own experience of meeting The Queen in 1997, when she came to open a new hostel for young homeless people that I was managing. I showed her round and introduced her to all the residents. I had expected it to be quite formal and awkward but I remember how adept she was at talking to such a diverse range of people."

4) The Queen speaks about Jesus

"This is the time of year when we remember that God sent his only son 'to serve, not to be served'. He restored love and service to the centre of our lives in the person of Jesus Christ." (2012)

"God sent into the world a unique person – neither a philosopher nor a general ... but a Saviour, with the power to forgive." (2011)

The Queen talks directly about the person at the heart of Christmas, the reason for celebrating. That includes both the example and achievement of Jesus and makes orthodox theology accessible to the widest possible audience.

5) The Queen speaks about faith in action

"Forgiveness lies at the heart of the Christian faith. It can heal broken families, it can restore friendships and it can reconcile divided communities. It is in forgiveness that we feel the power of God's love." (2011)

"For Christians, as for all people of faith, reflection, meditation and prayer help us to renew ourselves in God's love, as we strive daily to become better people." (2013)

Reconciliation, service and love flow from Christian commitment. The Queen talks about what faith *does.* It makes a difference to how we live and helps us to be 'better people'.

Quotations from The Queen's Christmas broadcasts, the excerpts in this book, cover many great themes of Christian faith and life. I have compiled them into major themes. The themes, of course, overlap and intertwine. Some quotations could fit into various themes, so I locate them in an obvious one.

These excerpts are samples or examples of the many themes and topics covered in around 70 broadcasts during The Queen's long reign. They are, in every case, part of a longer statement which gives them fuller significance. Nevertheless, they remain valuable insights and important messages about Christian beliefs and practices.

Queen Elizabeth II has been Queen of the United Kingdom, Australia, Canada, and New Zealand since 6 February 1952. She is

Queen of 12 countries that became independent since 1952, and is Head of the Commonwealth of Nations, a free association of independent member nations (commonly known as *the Commonwealth*), comprising over 50 sovereign states. The Queen carries the blessings and responsibilities of her reign with grace and dignity. She understands the value of influence, symbols, tradition and innovation.

Elizabeth II (born 21 April 1926) began her reign at the age of 25 when her father King George VI died. The Queen heard of her Accession while visiting Kenya.

Her first Christmas message, broadcast from the same desk and chair used by her father and grandfather, continued the tradition of Christmas Broadcasts passed on to her by George V and George VI. The Queen thanked her people for their loyalty and affection in the first months of her reign.

The Queen spoke about her forthcoming Coronation where she would dedicate herself anew to serve her people, concluding:

I want to ask you all, whatever your religion may be, to pray for me on that day - to pray that God may give me wisdom and strength to carry out the solemn promises I shall be making, and that I may faithfully serve Him and you, all the days of my life. May God bless and guide you all through the coming year. (1952)

Although many have commented on the strong Christian messages included in The Queen's Christmas broadcasts from 2000, this book shows that the previous fifty years also contained many clear references to the significance of Christmas as a celebration of the birth of Jesus Christ and his immeasurable influence in history and in billions of lives.

Christians of all nations and races believe the eternal truth of God's love of all people in the whole world as clearly expressed in one of the most famous passages in the Bible: "**For God so loved the world that he gave his only Son, so that everyone who believes** in him may not perish but may have eternal life" (John 3:16 NRSV).

The following pages give you brief quotations about the significance and meaning of Christmas and of Christian faith and life, drawn from The Queen's annual Christmas Broadcasts and from Her Majesty's historic 2020 Easter message, commemorating the baby born King, and his life, death, and resurrection – the King of kings and Lord of lords.

The Queen's quotations are printed in **_bold italic_** in this book.

Part 1

Key Statements on each theme

Key statements on each theme

Queen Elizabeth II regularly referred to many great themes of the Christian faith. This book gathers those comments from Her Majesty's annual broadcasts into the ten themes of Jesus Christ, service and support, faith and hope, light and life, love and kindness, truth and courage, peace and good will, compassion and care, forgiveness and reconciliation, and respect and tolerance.

These themes are central to Christian life and faith. Part 1 of this book gives a key statement on each theme drawn from Her Majesty's broadcasts. Part 2 compiles all the excerpts from 70 broadcasts arranged in these themes.

The excerpts, of course, mostly relate to Christmas but also give important insights into Christian faith.

Jesus Christ himself stands at the heart of Christian faith. That title, Jesus Christ, is drawn from words meaning Saviour and Messiah. His life, death, and resurrection are unique. Our calendars and diaries date from the time of his birth over 2000 years ago and Christmas is the annual celebration of his birth.

Service and support are key elements of living the Christian life and of life in general. Jesus "did not come to be served, but to serve, and to give his life as a ransom for many." Jesus is our example of service and support, especially for those in need.

Faith and hope spring eternal in the good news about Jesus Christ. Jesus often emphasized the importance of believing in God and of trusting in him for life now and for eternal life.

Light and life shine radiantly in the story of Jesus Christ. He is "the Light of the world" and he came to give life in all its fullness, abundant life. Millions now choose to live in that light and life.

Love and kindness flood through the life of Jesus, demonstrated most powerfully in his death and resurrection. Jesus' showed unconditional love and acceptance for all people.

Truth and courage characterized Jesus' life and teaching. He confronted and challenged hypocrisy and evil, declaring that he is "the way, the truth, and the life." His courage led him to his brutal death on a cross and his ultimate triumph over death.

Peace and goodwill toward all on earth were announced by angels at Jesus' birth. Our broken world needs that. Jesus gave his peace and on the eve of his execution he promised his peace even amid opposition and difficulties.

Compassion and care fill the story of Jesus and those who follow him faithfully. His compassion for the outcast, the sick, the despised, and the weak is legendary. He cared, and his actions demonstrated his compassion and care.

Forgiveness and reconciliation also flood through the life and teaching of Jesus. He did not come to judge but to love and to forgive, and he calls us to live that way also. Then we can enjoy harmony and live in reconciliation with one another.

Respect and tolerance can be found in living together in the harmony of mutual acceptance. We all differ, but our differences can enrich our lives and our understanding of one another. Jesus Christ mixed freely with all kinds of people in all levels of society and demonstrated acceptance, forgiveness, and love.

The flowing excerpts from The Queen's annual broadcasts give you her description of the meaning of Christmas and they indicate the importance and influence of Jesus' life and teaching.

The Queen describes the significance of Christmas and of the Christian faith while also acknowledging the importance of respecting people of all faiths and of none.

The ten excerpts in this first section give you key statements about each of the themes compiled in this book.

All these excerpts from The Queen's broadcasts are reproduced in this section and throughout this book in ***bold italic.***

1 Jesus Christ

Christmas broadcast 2000

The Queen's speech in 2000 dresribed the significance of the millennium.

Christmas is the traditional, if not the actual, birthday of a man who was destined to change the course of our history. And today we are celebrating the fact that Jesus Christ was born two thousand years ago; this is the true Millennium anniversary.

The simple facts of Jesus' life give us little clue as to the influence he was to have on the world. As a boy he learnt his father's trade as a carpenter. He then became a preacher, recruiting twelve supporters to help him.

But his ministry only lasted a few years and he himself never wrote anything down. In his early thirties he was arrested, tortured and crucified with two criminals. His death might have been the end of the story, but then came the resurrection and with it the foundation of the Christian faith.

Even in our very material age the impact of Christ's life is all around us. If you want to see an expression of Christian faith you have only to look at our awe-inspiring cathedrals and abbeys, listen to their music, or look at their stained glass windows, their books and their pictures.

But the true measure of Christ's influence is not only in the lives of the saints but also in the good works quietly done by millions of men and women day in and day out throughout the centuries.

Many will have been inspired by Jesus' simple but powerful teaching: love God and love thy neighbour as thyself - in other words, treat others as you would like them to treat you. His great emphasis was to give spirituality a practical purpose. ...

To many of us our beliefs are of fundamental importance. For me the teachings of Christ and my own personal accountability before God provide a framework in which I try to lead my life. I, like so many of you, have drawn great comfort in difficult times from Christ's words and example.

I believe that the Christian message, in the words of a familiar blessing, remains profoundly important to us all:

"Go forth into the world in peace,
be of good courage,
hold fast that which is good,
render to no man evil for evil,
strengthen the faint-hearted,
support the weak,
help the afflicted,
honour all men."

It is a simple message of compassion... and yet as powerful as ever today, two thousand years after Christ's birth. (2000)

31

2 Service & Support

Princess Elizabeth's 21st Birthday Speech, 21 April 1947

There is a motto which has been borne by many of my ancestors - a noble motto, "I serve". ...

I declare before you all that my whole life whether it be long or short shall be devoted to your service and the service of our great imperial family to which we all belong.

But I shall not have strength to carry out this resolution alone unless you join in it with me, as I now invite you to do: I know that your support will be unfailingly given. God help me to make good my vow, and God bless all of you who are willing to share in it. (1947, Princess Elizabeth at 21)

3 Faith & Hope

Golden Jubilee Australian commemorative stamps 2002

Anniversaries are important events in all our lives. Christmas is the anniversary of the birth of Christ over two thousand years ago, but it is much more than that. It is the celebration of the birth of an idea and an ideal. ...

I know just how much I rely on my own faith to guide me through the good times and the bad. Each day is a new beginning, I know that the only way to live my life is to try to do what is right, to take the long view, to give of my best in all that the day brings, and to put my trust in God.

Like others of you who draw inspiration from your own faith, I draw strength from the message of hope in the Christian gospel.

Fortified by this and the support you have given throughout the last twelve months which has meant so much to me, I look forward to the New Year, to facing the challenges and opportunities that lie ahead, and to continuing to serve you to the very best of my ability each and every day. (2002)

4 Light & Life

Candlelight from the Easter Message

As darkness falls on the Saturday before Easter Day, many Christians would normally light candles together. In church, one light would pass to another, spreading slowly and then more rapidly as more candles are lit. It's a way of showing how the good news of Christ's resurrection has been passed on from the first Easter by every generation until now.

This year, Easter will be different for many of us, but by keeping apart we keep others safe. But Easter isn't cancelled; indeed, we need Easter as much as ever. The discovery of the risen Christ on the first Easter Day gave his followers new hope and fresh purpose, and we can all take heart from this. We know that Coronavirus will not overcome us. As dark as death can be — particularly for those suffering with grief — light and life are greater. May the living flame of the Easter hope be a steady guide as we face the future.

5 Love & Kindness

Earth from space, NASA

The Queen said that **technical skills are not enough by themselves. They can only come to the rescue of the planet if we also learn to live by the golden rule which Jesus Christ taught us - "love thy neighbour as thyself".**

Many of you will have heard the story of the Good Samaritan, and of how Christ answered the question (from a clever lawyer who was trying to catch him out) "Who is my neighbour?"

Jesus told of the traveller who was mugged and left injured on the roadside where several important people saw him, and passed by without stopping to help.

His neighbour was the man who did stop, cared for him, and made sure he was being well looked after before he resumed his own journey. ...

You children have something to give us which is priceless. You can still look at the world with a sense of wonder and remind us grown-ups that life is wonderful and precious. Often a child's helplessness and vulnerability bring out the best in us. (1989)

6 Truth & Courage

The first televised Royal Christmas Message, 1957

Twenty-five years ago my grandfather broadcast the first of these Christmas messages. Today is another landmark because television has made it possible for many of you to see me in your homes on Christmas Day. I very much hope that this new medium will make my Christmas message more personal and direct.

I believe in our qualities and in our strength, I believe that together we can set an example to the world which will encourage upright people everywhere.

I would like to read you a few lines from 'Pilgrim's Progress', because I am sure we can say with Mr Valiant for Truth, these words:

"Though with great difficulty I am got hither, yet now I do not repent me of all the trouble I have been at to arrive where I am. My sword I give to him that shall succeed me in my pilgrimage and my courage and skill to him that can get it. My marks and scars I carry with me, to be a witness for me that I have fought his battles who now will be my rewarder." (1957)

7 Peace & Goodwill

The first Royal Christmas Message televised in colour, 1967

Modern communications make it possible for me to talk to you in your homes and to wish you a merry Christmas and a very happy New Year. These techniques of radio and television are modern, but the Christmas message is timeless.

You may have heard it very often but in the end, no matter what scientific progress we make, the message will count for nothing unless we can achieve real peace and encourage genuine goodwill between individual people and the nations of the world.

Every Christmas I am sustained and encouraged by the happiness and sense of unity which comes from seeing all the members of my family together.

I hope and pray that, with God's help, this Christmas spirit of family unity will spread and grow among our Commonwealth family of nations. (1967)

8 Compassion & Care

Diamond Wedding Anniversary 2007

Now today, of course, marks the birth of Jesus Christ. Among other things, it is a reminder that it is the story of a family; but of a family in very distressed circumstances. Mary and Joseph found no room at the inn; they had to make do in a stable, and the new-born Jesus had to be laid in a manger. This was a family which had been shut out.

Perhaps it was because of this early experience that, throughout his ministry, Jesus of Nazareth reached out and made friends with people whom others ignored or despised. It was in this way that he proclaimed his belief that, in the end, we are all brothers and sisters in one human family.

The Christmas story also draws attention to all those people who are on the edge of society - people who feel cut off and disadvantaged; people who, for one reason or another, are not able to enjoy the full benefits of living in a civilised and law-abiding community. For these people the modern world can seem a distant and hostile place. (2007)

9 Forgiveness & Reconciliation

'Reconciliation' by Josefina de Vasconcellos at Coventry Cathedral

In the ruins of the old Coventry Cathedral is a sculpture of a man and a woman reaching out to embrace each other ... inspired by the story of a woman who crossed Europe on foot after the war to find her husband.

For me, the life of Jesus Christ, the Prince of Peace, whose birth we celebrate today, is an inspiration and an anchor in my life.

A role model of reconciliation and forgiveness, he stretched out his hands in love, acceptance and healing. Christ's example has taught me to seek to respect and value all people, of whatever faith or none.

Sometimes it seems that reconciliation stands little chance in the face of war and discord. But, as the Christmas truce a century ago reminds us, peace and goodwill have lasting power in the hearts of men and women. (2014)

10 Respect & Tolerance

Remembrance Day

From time to time we also see some inspiring examples of tolerance. Mr Gordon Wilson, whose daughter Marie lost her life in the horrifying explosion at Enniskillen on Remembrance Sunday, impressed the whole world by the depth of his forgiveness.

His strength, and that of his wife, and the courage of their daughter, came from their Christian conviction. All of us will echo their prayer that out of the personal tragedies of Enniskillen may come a reconciliation between the communities. ...

I am afraid that the Christmas message of goodwill has usually evaporated by the time Boxing Day is over. This year I hope we will continue to remember the many innocent victims of violence and intolerance and the suffering of their families. Christians are taught to love their neighbours, not just at Christmas, but all the year round. (1987)

Part 2

The Statements
on each theme

Part 2: The Statements on each theme, compiles quotes and excerpts from all of The Queen's speeches throughout Her Majesty's long reign.

They include quotations on these themes:

1 Jesus Christ

2 Service & Support

3 Faith & Hope

4 Light & Life

5 Love & Kindness

6 Truth & Courage

7 Peace & Goodwill

8 Compassion & Care

9 Forgiveness & Reconciliation

10 Respect & Tolerance

Many quotations could fit into more than one of these categories so they are included here in an obvious theme expressed in the excerpt.

Quotations

The Queen's
Christmas & Easter
Messages

Queen Elizabeth II describes the
significance of Christmas & Easter

Geoffrey Waugh

Quotations in this book, in **bold italic print,** are reproduced
from my book *The Queen's Christmas & Easter Messages*, and
from the broadcast scripts in the Royal Family website
(https://www.royal.uk) with excerpts used by permission.

1 Jesus Christ

Jesus Christ himself stands at the heart of Christian faith. That title, Jesus Christ, is drawn from words meaning Saviour and Messiah. His life, death, and resurrection are unique. Our calendars and diaries date from the time of his birth over 2000 years ago and Christmas is the annual celebration of his birth.

Christians believe that God walked among us in the person of his one and only Son, miraculously born of a virgin, with God his true Father. Jesus said, "I and the Father are one," and "If you have seen me, you have seen the Father."

He showed and taught us about God's love and justice, making people whole physically and spiritually. He promised eternal life to all who in trust him, and publicly died an excruciating death in our place, as our Saviour and Lord. Millions now trust him and follow his teaching and example.

His short life and even shorter three years of public ministry and service demonstrated God's love, acceptance, forgiveness and grace for us all.

Dr James Allan Francis paints a vivid picture, often quoted and adapted as 'One Solitary Life' [*The Real Jesus and Other Sermons,* Judson Press, 1926, pp 123-124.]

> A child is born in an obscure village. He is brought up in another obscure village. He works in a carpenter shop until he is thirty, and then for three brief years is an itinerant preacher, proclaiming a message and living a life. He never writes a book. He never holds an office. He never raises an army. He never has a family of his own. He never owns a home. He never goes to college. He never travels two hundred miles from the place where he was born. He gathers a little group of friends about him and teaches them his way of life. While still a young man, the tide of popular feeling turns against him. One denies him; another betrays

him. He is turned over to his enemies. He goes through the mockery of a trial; he is nailed to a cross between two thieves, and when dead is laid in a borrowed grave by the kindness of a friend.

Those are the facts of his human life. He rises from the dead. Today we look back across nineteen hundred years and ask, What kind of trail has he left across the centuries? When we try to sum up his influence, all the armies that ever marched, all the parliaments that ever sat, all the kings that ever reigned are absolutely picayune in their influence on mankind compared with that of this one solitary life.

Queen Elizabeth II spoke often about Jesus Christ in her broadcasts including these brief quotations.

Christ not only revealed to us the truth in his teachings. He lived by what he believed and gave us the strength to try to do the same - and, finally, on the cross, he showed the supreme example of physical and moral courage. (1981)

Many will have been inspired by Jesus' simple but powerful teaching: love God and love thy neighbour as thyself - in other words, treat others as you would like them to treat you. His great emphasis was to give spirituality a practical purpose. (2000)

Jesus Christ lived obscurely for most of his life, and never travelled far. He was maligned and rejected by many, though he had done no wrong. And yet, billions of people now follow his teaching and find in him the guiding light for their lives. I am one of them because Christ's example helps me see the value of doing small things with great love, whoever does them and whatever they themselves believe. (2016)

Quotations about Jesus Christ

The Queen's first Christmas Broadcast 1952

Each Christmas, at this time, my beloved father broadcast a message to his people in all parts of the world. Today I am doing this to you, who are now my people.

As he used to do, I am speaking to you from my own home, where I am spending Christmas with my family; and let me say at once how I hope that your children are enjoying themselves as much as mine are on a day which is especially the children's festival, kept in honour of the Child born at Bethlehem nearly two thousand years ago. ...

Above all, we must keep alive that courageous spirit of adventure that is the finest quality of youth; and by youth I do not just mean those who are young in years; I mean too all those who are young in heart, no matter how old they may be. That spirit still flourishes in this old country and in all the younger countries of our Commonwealth.

On this broad foundation let us set out to build a truer knowledge of ourselves and our fellowmen, to work for tolerance and understanding among the nations and to use the tremendous forces of science and learning for the betterment of man's lot upon this earth. If we can do these three things with courage, with generosity and with humility, then surely we shall achieve that "Peace on earth, Goodwill toward men" which is the eternal message of Christmas, and the desire of us all. (1952)

That eternal message of Christmas, and the desire of us all, stems from the birth, life, death, and resurrection of that baby heralded by the angels.

As human beings we generally know what is right and how we should act and speak. But we are also very aware of how difficult it is to have the courage of our convictions.

Our Christian faith helps us to sustain those convictions. Christ not only revealed to us the truth in his teachings. He lived by what he believed and gave us the strength to try to do the same - and, finally, on the cross, he showed the supreme example of physical and moral courage.

That sacrifice was the dawn of Christianity and this is why at Christmas time we are inspired by the example of Christ as we celebrate his birth. (1981)

In 1986 The Queen gave a longer reflection on the significance of Christmas.

Christmas is a festival for all Christians, but it is particularly a festival for children. As we all know, it commemorates the birth of a child, who was born to ordinary people, and who grew up very simply in his own small home town and was trained to be a carpenter.

47

His life thus began in humble surroundings, in fact in a stable, but he was to have a profound influence on the course of history, and on the lives of generations of his followers. You don't have to be rich or powerful in order to change things for the better and each of us in our own way can make a contribution.

The infant Jesus was fortunate in one very important respect. His parents were loving and considerate. They did their utmost to protect him from harm. They left their own home and became refugees, to save him from King Herod, and they brought him up according to the traditions of their faith.

Christmas stamps 1986

It is no easy task to care for and bring up children, whatever your circumstances - whether you are famous or quite unknown. But we could all help by letting the spirit of Christmas fill our homes with love and care and by heeding Our Lord's injunction to treat others as you would like them to treat you.

When, as the Bible says, Christ grew in wisdom and understanding, he began his task of explaining and teaching just what it is that God wants from us.

The two lessons that he had for us, which he underlined in everything he said and did, are the messages of God's love and how essential it is that we, too, should love other people.

There are many serious and threatening problems in this country and in the world but they will never be solved until there is peace in our homes and love in our hearts.

The message which God sent us by Christ's life and example is a very simple one, even though it seems so difficult to put into practice.

To all of you, of every faith and race, I send you my best wishes for a time of peace and tranquillity with your families at this Festival of Christmas. A very Happy Christmas to you all.
(1986)

The 1988 Christmas Speech commented on the *'Book of Hours',* *full of prayers and devotional readings,* with detailed illustrations such as this collage of the Christmas story.

Book of Hours segment from the TV broadcast 1988

Recalling anniversaries, The Queen said that *we surely should draw inspiration from one other anniversary - the one we celebrate every year at this time, the birth of Christ.*

There are many grand and splendid pictures in the Royal Collection that illustrate this event, but one which gives me particular pleasure is this precious, almost jewel-like book.

It is a 'Book of Hours', full of prayers and devotional readings. It's in Latin, but it contains the most exquisite illuminations and it is these that speak to us most movingly. The anonymous person who drew the pictures nearly five hundred years ago has included all the familiar elements of the Christmas story which we hear with such pleasure every year.

Here are the angels, bringing the glad tidings to the shepherds, who listen attentively. Down here, where baby Jesus lies in the stall, you can see Mary and Joseph, watching over him, quite unmoved, it seems, by the man playing the bagpipes overhead.

The star over the stable has lit the way for all of us ever since, and there should be no one who feels shut out from that welcoming and guiding light. The legends of Christmas about the ox and the ass suggest that even the animals are not outside that loving care. ...

May the Christmas story encourage you, for it is a message of hope every year, not for a few, but for all. (1988)

The Queen Mother at 100 in 2000 with The Queen and Princess Margaret

The Queen's speech in 2000 reflected on the significance of the millennium.

Christmas is the traditional, if not the actual, birthday of a man who was destined to change the course of our history. And today we are celebrating the fact that Jesus Christ was born two thousand years ago; this is the true Millennium anniversary.

The simple facts of Jesus' life give us little clue as to the influence he was to have on the world. As a boy he learnt his father's trade as a carpenter. He then became a preacher, recruiting twelve supporters to help him.

But his ministry only lasted a few years and he himself never wrote anything down. In his early thirties he was arrested, tortured and crucified with two criminals. His death might have been the end of the story, but then came the resurrection and with it the foundation of the Christian faith.

Even in our very material age the impact of Christ's life is all around us. If you want to see an expression of Christian faith you have only to look at our awe-inspiring cathedrals and abbeys, listen to their music, or look at their stained glass windows, their books and their pictures.

But the true measure of Christ's influence is not only in the lives of the saints but also in the good works quietly done by millions of men and women day in and day out throughout the centuries.

Many will have been inspired by Jesus' simple but powerful teaching: love God and love thy neighbour as thyself - in other words, treat others as you would like them to treat you. His great emphasis was to give spirituality a practical purpose. ...

To many of us our beliefs are of fundamental importance. For me the teachings of Christ and my own personal accountability before God provide a framework in which I try to lead my life. I, like so many of you, have drawn great comfort in difficult times from Christ's words and example.

I believe that the Christian message, in the words of a familiar blessing, remains profoundly important to us all:

"Go forth into the world in peace,
be of good courage,
hold fast that which is good,
render to no man evil for evil,
strengthen the faint-hearted,
support the weak,
help the afflicted,
honour all men."

It is a simple message of compassion... and yet as powerful as ever today, two thousand years after Christ's birth. (2000)

The Queen at 90 reflected on the influence of Jesus Christ.

United Kingdom commemorative stamps 2016

At Christmas our attention is drawn to the birth of a baby some two thousand years ago. It was the humblest of beginnings, and his parents, Joseph and Mary, did not think they were important.

Jesus Christ lived obscurely for most of his life, and never travelled far. He was maligned and rejected by many, though he had done no wrong. And yet, billions of people now follow his teaching and find in him the guiding light for their lives. I am one of them because Christ's example helps me see the value of doing small things with great love, whoever does them and whatever they themselves believe.

The message of Christmas reminds us that inspiration is a gift to be given as well as received, and that love begins small but always grows. (2016)

2 Service & Support

Service and support are key elements of living a compassionate life. Jesus Christ "did not come to be served, but to serve, and to give his life as a ransom for many." Jesus is our great example of service and support, especially for those in need.

Jesus lived a life of service and sacrifice. He challenged his followers to do the same. When his disciples argued about who was greatest he reminded them that the greatest was the servant of all. Even during his last meal with them before he was arrested and executed, his disciples argued about who was greatest. Jesus laid aside his garments, wrapped a towel around himself and washed their dusty feet, dressed as a lowly servant, to their astonishment and objection. He reminded them that as their Lord and Master he had served them, and that they must serve one another.

He grew up in the green hills of Nazareth working as a carpenter and the son of a carpenter in the family business. That work involved building and repairing houses and furniture including working with the limestone used in most buildings, and felling needed timber. Jesus grew in strength and in favour with God and people. As the eldest with four brothers and his sisters he also grew in family responsibilities and serving ability.

Then, following his baptism at around thirty years old, he began his intensive public service, meeting the needs of people every day. Large crowds came for healing and help and his teaching astonished many people. He emphasized that the greatest must be the servant of all, that the first would be last and the last first.

He continually taught about serving and supporting others, loving others, helping others, and accepting and forgiving others. His famous teaching included powerful stories such as 'The Good

Samaritan' (a people despised) helping the wounded traveller, and 'The Prodigal Son' fully and freely forgiven and restored.

Mahatma Gandhi, the revered Hindu leader in India is reported to have said, "I like your Christ, I do not like your Christians. Your Christians are so unlike your Christ." Similar to Christ's teaching he said, "Hate the sin, love the sinner" and "The best way to find yourself is to lose yourself in the service of others."

The Queen spoke often about service as in these quotes:

The Founder of the Christian Faith himself chose twelve disciples to help him in his ministry.

In this country and throughout the Commonwealth there are groups of people who are giving their time generously to make a difference to the lives of others. (2003)

This is the time of year when we remember that God sent his only son 'to serve, not to be served'. He restored love and service to the centre of our lives in the person of Jesus Christ.

It is my prayer this Christmas Day that his example and teaching will continue to bring people together to give the best of themselves in the service of others.

The carol, In The Bleak Midwinter, ends by asking a question of all of us who know the Christmas story, of how God gave himself to us in humble service: 'What can I give him, poor as I am? If I were a shepherd, I would bring a lamb; if I were a wise man, I would do my part'. The carol gives the answer 'Yet what I can I give him - give my heart'. (2012)

Quotations about Service and Support

Princess Elizabeth's 21st Birthday Speech 21 Apr 1947

I declare before you all that my whole life whether it be long or short shall be devoted to your service and the service of our great imperial family to which we all belong.

But I shall not have strength to carry out this resolution alone unless you join in it with me, as I now invite you to do: I know that your support will be unfailingly given. God help me to make good my vow, and God bless all of you who are willing to share in it. (1947, Princess Elizabeth at 21)

Telstar in 1962 made instant global communication possible.

The wise men of old followed a star: modern man has built one. But unless the message of this new star is the same as theirs our wisdom will count for nought. Now we can all say the world is my neighbour and it is only in serving one another that we can reach for the stars. (1962)

The 1980 broadcast reflected on the celebrations of the 80th birthday of Queen Elizabeth The Queen Mother and addressed the theme of service.

I was glad that the celebrations of my mother's 80th birthday last summer gave so much pleasure. I wonder whether you remember, during the Thanksgiving Service in St. Paul's, the congregation singing that wonderful hymn "Immortal, Invisible, God only wise".

"Now give us we pray thee the Spirit of love,
The gift of true wisdom that comes from above,
The spirit of service that has naught of pride,
The gift of true courage, and thee as our guide." ...

In difficult times we may be tempted to find excuses for self-indulgence and to wash our hands of responsibility. Christmas stands for the opposite. The Wise Men and the Shepherds remind us that it is not enough simply to do our jobs; we need to go out and look for opportunities to help those less fortunate than ourselves, even if that service demands sacrifice.

It was their belief and confidence in God which inspired them to visit the stable and it is this unselfish will to serve that will see us through the difficulties we face.

We know that the world can never be free from conflict and pain, but Christmas also draws our attention to all that is hopeful and good in this changing world; it speaks of values and qualities that are true and permanent and it reminds us that the world we would like to see can only come from the goodness of the heart. (1980)

Those true and permanent values are seen in sacrificial service to others.

Curiously enough, it was a sad event which did as much as anything in 1992 to help me put my own worries into perspective. Just before he died, Leonard Cheshire came to see us with his fellow members of the Order of Merit. ...

One of his Cheshire Homes for people with disabilities is not far from this house. I have visited others all over the Commonwealth and I have seen at first hand the remarkable results of his, and his wife's, determination to put Christ's teaching to practical effect. ...

There is no magic formula that will transform sorrow into happiness, intolerance into compassion or war into peace, but inspiration can change human behaviour.

Those, like Leonard Cheshire, who devote their lives to others, have that inspiration and they know, and we know, where to look for help in finding it. That help can be readily given if we only have the faith to ask.

I and my family, as we approach a new year, will draw strength from this faith in our commitment to your service in the coming years. (1992)

The Queen often commented on the quiet service of millions of people.

My work, and the work of my family, takes us every week into that quiet sort of 'public life', where millions of people give their time, unpaid and usually unsung, to the community, and indeed to those most at risk of exclusion from it. ...

It is they that help define our sense of duty. It is they that can make us strong as individuals, and keep the nation's heartbeat strong and steady too. Christmas is a good time for us to recognise all that they do for us and to say a heartfelt thank you to each and every one of them. (1999)

Jesus also demonstrated sacrificial service and taught it.

The Founder of the Christian Faith himself chose twelve disciples to help him in his ministry.

In this country and throughout the Commonwealth there are groups of people who are giving their time generously to make a difference to the lives of others.

As we think of them, and of our Servicemen and women far from home at this Christmas time, I hope we all, whatever our faith, can draw inspiration from the words of the familiar prayer:

"Teach us good Lord
To serve thee as thou deservest;
To give, and not to count the cost;
To fight, and not to heed the wounds;
To toil, and not to seek for rest;
To labour, and not to ask for any reward;
Save that of knowing that we do thy will."
(2003)

First Christmas Broadcast in 3D, 2012

At Christmas I am always struck by how the spirit of togetherness lies also at the heart of the Christmas story. A young mother and a dutiful father with their baby were joined by poor shepherds and visitors from afar. They came with their gifts to worship the Christ child. From that day on he has inspired people to commit themselves to the best interests of others.

This is the time of year when we remember that God sent his only son 'to serve, not to be served'. He restored love and service to the centre of our lives in the person of Jesus Christ.

It is my prayer this Christmas Day that his example and teaching will continue to bring people together to give the best of themselves in the service of others.

The carol, In The Bleak Midwinter, ends by asking a question of all of us who know the Christmas story, of how God gave himself to us in humble service: 'What can I give him, poor as I am? If I were a shepherd, I would bring a lamb; if I were a wise man, I would do my part'. The carol gives the answer 'Yet what I can I give him - give my heart'. (2012)

3 Faith & Hope

Faith and hope spring eternal in the good news about Jesus Christ. Jesus often emphasized the importance of believing in God and of trusting in him for life now and for eternal life.

Jesus encouraged us to have faith in God and also in him. Even during his last meal with his followers on the night before he died he challenged them, "Believe in God, believe also in me."

That simple, profound faith gives a believer hope now and hope for the future including for our eternal destiny.

Jesus often said, "Your faith has made you whole." He was especially impressed with anyone who had strong faith in him such as a Roman centurion who sent a message to Jesus affirming, "Just say the word and my servant will be healed." That sick servant was healed and Jesus praised the Roman for his simple, strong faith in him.

Faith and hope in God are simple and also profound. Millions believe that God exists and that his Son Jesus was incarnate on earth and died on our behalf for the forgiveness of our sin.

Christmas is the celebration of Jesus Christ's birth as The Queen continually reminded us in her annual broadcasts. That miraculous birth gives us hope as we have faith. Here are some of Her Majesty's statements.

Every year at this time the whole Christian world celebrates the birth of the founder of our faith. ...

The story is of a poor man and his wife who took refuge at night in a stable, where a child was born and laid in the manger. Nothing very spectacular, and yet the event was greeted with that triumphant song: "Glory to God in the highest, and on earth peace, goodwill towards men."

For that child was to show that there is nothing in heaven and earth that cannot be achieved by faith and by love and service to one's neighbour. (1961)

Christ's birth in Bethlehem so long ago remains a powerful symbol of hope for a better future. After all the tribulations of this year, this is surely more relevant than ever. (2001)

I know just how much I rely on my own faith to guide me through the good times and the bad. Each day is a new beginning, I know that the only way to live my life is to try to do what is right, to take the long view, to give of my best in all that the day brings, and to put my trust in God.

Like others of you who draw inspiration from your own faith, I draw strength from the message of hope in the Christian gospel. (2002)

Of course, at the heart of the Christmas story lies the birth of a child, a seemingly small and insignificant step overlooked by many in Bethlehem. But in time, through his teaching and by his example, Jesus Christ would show the world how small steps, taken in faith and in hope, can overcome long-held differences and deep-seated divisions to bring harmony and understanding. (2019)

Quotations about Faith and Hope

Australian commemorative stamps, 2 June 2003

In her coronation year The Queen observed that the Commonwealth *is an entirely new conception, built on the highest qualities of the spirit of man: friendship, loyalty and the desire for freedom and peace.*

To that new conception of an equal partnership of nations and races I shall give myself heart and soul every day of my life.

I wished to speak of it from New Zealand this Christmas Day because we are celebrating the birth of the Prince of Peace, who preached the brotherhood of man.

May that brotherhood be furthered by all our thoughts and deeds from year to year. In pursuit of that supreme ideal the Commonwealth is moving steadily towards greater harmony between its many creeds, colours and races despite the imperfections by which, like every human institution, it is beset.

Already, indeed, in the last half-century it has proved itself the most effective and progressive association of peoples which history has yet seen; and its ideal of brotherhood embraces the whole world. To all my peoples throughout the Commonwealth I commend that Christmas hope and prayer. (1953)

Every year at this time the whole Christian world celebrates the birth of the founder of our faith. It is traditionally the time for family reunions, present-giving and children's parties.

A welcome escape, in fact, from the harsh realities of this troubled world and it is just in times like these, times of tension and anxieties, that the simple story and message of Christmas is most relevant.

The story is of a poor man and his wife who took refuge at night in a stable, where a child was born and laid in the manger. Nothing very spectacular, and yet the event was greeted with that triumphant song: "Glory to God in the highest, and on earth peace, goodwill towards men."

For that child was to show that there is nothing in heaven and earth that cannot be achieved by faith and by love and service to one's neighbour. Christmas may be a Christian festival, but its message goes out to all men and it is echoed by all men of understanding and goodwill everywhere. ...

"Oh hush the noise, ye men of strife, and hear the angels sing." The words of this old carol mean even more today than when they were first written. (1961)

New hope and new confidence arise from the coming of Jesus.

At Christmas, we look back nearly 2000 years to an event which was to bring new hope and new confidence to all subsequent generations.

The birth of Christ gave us faith in the future and as I read through some earlier Christmas Broadcasts, I was struck by the way that this same idea - faith in the future - kept recurring. ...

The optimism of that Christmas message is timeless. When it first fell to me to carry on the tradition that my grandfather and father had developed, I reaffirmed what I knew had been their deeply held beliefs in the future, beliefs which I myself share. ...

Christians have the compelling example of the life and teaching of Christ and, for myself, I would like nothing more than that my grandchildren should hold dear his ideals which have helped and inspired so many previous generations. (1978)

We celebrate a child who transformed history.

At Christmas we give presents to each other. Let us also stop to think whether we are making enough effort to pass on our experience of life to our children. Today we celebrate the birth of the child who transformed history and gave us a great faith. Jesus said:

"Suffer the little children to come unto me and forbid them not, for of such is the kingdom of God". (1978)

Following the 11 September (9/11) attack in 2001 The Queen observed:

It is to the Church that we turn to give meaning to these moments of intense human experience through prayer, symbol and ceremony.

In these circumstances so many of us, whatever our religion, need our faith more than ever to sustain and guide us. Every one of us needs to believe in the value of all that is good and honest; we need to let this belief drive and influence our actions. ...

This is an important lesson for us all during this festive season. For Christmas marks a moment to pause, to reflect and believe in the possibilities of rebirth and renewal.

Christ's birth in Bethlehem so long ago remains a powerful symbol of hope for a better future. After all the tribulations of this year, this is surely more relevant than ever.

As we come together amongst family and friends and look forward to the coming year, I hope that in the months to come we shall be able to find ways of strengthening our own communities as a sure support and comfort to us all - whatever may lie ahead.

May I, in this my fiftieth Christmas message to you, once again wish every one of you a very happy Christmas. (2001)

Faith gives us the strength of hope in the future.

Golden Jubilee Australian commemorative stamps 2002

Anniversaries are important events in all our lives. Christmas is the anniversary of the birth of Christ over two thousand years ago, but it is much more than that. It is the celebration of the birth of an idea and an ideal. ...

I know just how much I rely on my own faith to guide me through the good times and the bad. Each day is a new beginning, I know that the only way to live my life is to try to do what is right, to take the long view, to give of my best in all that the day brings, and to put my trust in God.

Like others of you who draw inspiration from your own faith, I draw strength from the message of hope in the Christian gospel.

Fortified by this and the support you have given throughout the last twelve months which has meant so much to me, I look forward to the New Year, to facing the challenges and opportunities that lie ahead, and to continuing to serve you to the very best of my ability each and every day. (2002, the Golden Jubilee of The Queen's reign)

In the year ahead, I hope you will have time to pause for moments of quiet reflection. ...

For Christians, as for all people of faith, reflection, meditation and prayer help us to renew ourselves in God's love, as we strive daily to become better people. The Christmas message shows us that this love is for everyone. There is no one beyond its reach.

On the first Christmas, in the fields above Bethlehem, as they sat in the cold of night watching their resting sheep, the local shepherds must have had no shortage of time for reflection. Suddenly all this was to change. These humble shepherds were the first to hear and ponder the wondrous news of the birth of Christ – the first noel – the joy of which we celebrate today. (2013)

Small steps taken in faith and hope can bring harmony.

Of course, at the heart of the Christmas story lies the birth of a child, a seemingly small and insignificant step overlooked by many in Bethlehem. But in time, through his teaching and by his example, Jesus Christ would show the world how small steps, taken in faith and in hope, can overcome long-held differences and deep-seated divisions to bring harmony and understanding.

Many of us try to follow in his footsteps. The path, of course, is not always smooth, and may at times this year have felt quite bumpy. But small steps can make a world of difference.

As Christmas dawned, church congregations around the world joined in singing 'It Came upon the Midnight Clear'. Like many timeless carols, it speaks not just of the coming of Jesus Christ into a divided world many years ago, but also of the relevance even today of the angels' message of peace and goodwill.

It's a timely reminder of what positive things can be achieved when people set aside past differences and come together in the spirit of friendship and reconciliation. And as we all look forward to the start of a new decade, it's worth remembering that it is often the small steps, not the giant leaps, that bring about the most lasting change. (2019)

In 2005 The Queen reflected on tragedies such as the Boxing Day 2004 Indian Ocean tsunami, Hurricane Katrina and the floods in New Orleans, the earthquake in Kashmir which killed over 70,000 people and left millions homeless, and the July bombings in London killing underground commuters. Footage showed ordinary people helping the suffering in practical and financial ways in the remarkable humanitarian responses from people of all faiths.

This Christmas my thoughts are especially with those everywhere who are grieving the loss of loved ones during what for so many has been such a terrible year. ...

There may be an instinct in all of us to help those in distress, but in many cases I believe this has been inspired by religious faith. Christianity is not the only religion to teach its followers to help others and to treat your neighbour as you would want to be treated yourself.

It has been clear that in the course of this year relief workers and financial support have come from members of every faith and from every corner of the world. ...

This last year has reminded us that this world is not always an easy or a safe place to live in, but it is the only place we have. I believe also that it has shown us all how our faith - whatever our religion - can inspire us to work together in friendship and peace for the sake of our own and future generations.

For Christians this festival of Christmas is the time to remember the birth of the one we call "the Prince of Peace" and our source of "light and life" in both good times and bad. It is not always easy to accept his teaching, but I have no doubt that the New Year will be all the better if we do but try.

I hope you will all have a very happy Christmas this year and that you go into the New Year with renewed hope and confidence. (2005)

4 Light & Life

Light and life shine radiantly in the story of Jesus Christ. He is "the Light of the world" and he came to give life in all its fullness, abundant life. Millions now choose to live in that light and life.

Jesus claimed to be the light of the world and also added, "You are the light of the world. ... Let your light shine before others, so that they may see your good works and give glory to your Father in heaven" (Matthew 5:14, 16).

Scripture reminds us that Jesus Christ brought light and life into the world for "in him was life, and the life was the light of all people. The light shines in the darkness, and the darkness did not overcome it" (John 1:4-5).

Light dispels darkness and we are invited to live in the light of God's love and goodness and reflect his light and love. We can live in that light and love amid the darkness and evil around us.

Many people who have near death experiences consistently report that they were drawn into the wonderful presence of a great being of love and light. Christians affirm that God is love and that God is light and in him there is no darkness at all.

The Queen often referred to the original Christmas story of a unique baby born to a poor family who brought us light and life, as in these excerpts.

Life in such a place might have been uneventful. But the Light, kindled in Bethlehem and then streaming from the cottage window in Nazareth, has illumined the world for two thousand years. It is in the glow of that bright beam that I wish you all a blessed Christmas and a happy New Year. (1954)

The first Christmas came at a time that was dark and threatening, but from it came the light of the world. (1974)

I am reminded this year of some lines from a Christmas hymn which many of you will know: "Yet in thy dark streets shineth the everlasting light. The hopes and fears of all the years are met in thee tonight." (1993)

Light brings hope and life even during the Coronavirus pandemic.

Every year, we herald the coming of Christmas by turning on the lights. And light does more than create a festive mood. Light brings hope.

For Christians Jesus is "the light of the world" but we can't celebrate his birth today in quite the usual way. ...

The teachings of Christ have served as my inner light, as has the sense of purpose we can find in coming together to worship. ...

Let the light of Christmas, the spirit of selflessness, love, and above all hope, guide us in the times ahead. It is in that spirit I wish you a very happy Christmas. (2020)

Quotations about Light and Life

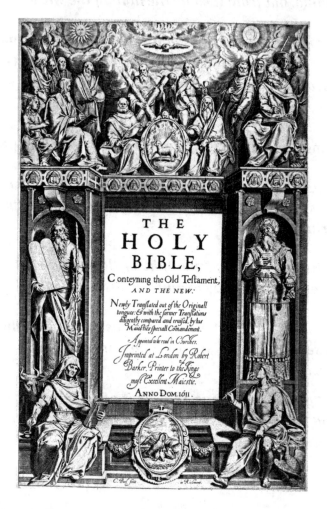

The title page to the 1611 first edition of the Authorized Version of the Bible shows the Apostles Peter and Paul seated centrally above the central text, which is flanked by Moses and Aaron. In the four corners sit Matthew, Mark, Luke and John, authors of the four gospels, with their symbolic animals. The rest of the Apostles (with Judas facing away) stand around Peter and Paul. At the very top is the Tetragrammaton "יְהֹוָה" [YHWH] in Hebrew diacritics.

Over four hundred years ago, King James the Sixth of Scotland inherited the throne of England at a time when the Christian Church was deeply divided. Here at Hampton Court in 1604, he convened a conference of churchmen of all shades of opinion to discuss the future of Christianity in this country. The King agreed to commission a new translation of the Bible that was acceptable to all parties. This was to become the King James or Authorized Bible, which next year will be exactly four centuries old.

Acknowledged as a masterpiece of English prose and the most vivid translation of the scriptures, the glorious language of this Bible has survived the turbulence of history and given many of us the most widely-recognised and beautiful descriptions of the birth of Jesus Christ which we celebrate today. ...

People are capable of belonging to many communities, including a religious faith. King James may not have anticipated quite how important sport and games were to become in promoting harmony and common interests. But from the scriptures in the Bible which bears his name, we know that nothing is more satisfying than the feeling of belonging to a group who are dedicated to helping each other:

'Therefore all things whatsoever ye would that men should to do to you, do ye even so to them'. [Matthew 7:12] (2010)

Light kindled in Bethlehem has illuminated the world.

I have referred to Christmas as the Children's Festival. But this lovely day is not only a time for family reunions, for paper decorations, for roast turkey and plum pudding.

It has, before all, its origin in the homage we pay to a very special Family, who lived long ago in a very ordinary home, in a very unimportant village in the uplands of a small Roman province.

Life in such a place might have been uneventful. But the Light, kindled in Bethlehem and then streaming from the cottage window in Nazareth, has illumined the world for two thousand years. It is in the glow of that bright beam that I wish you all a blessed Christmas and a happy New Year. (1954)

Christmas on this side of the equator comes at the darkest time of the year: but we can look forward hopefully to lengthening days and the returning sun.

The first Christmas came at a time that was dark and threatening, but from it came the light of the world. (1974)

I am always moved by those words in St. John's Gospel which we hear on Christmas Day - "He was in the world, and the world was made by him, and the world knew him not".

We have only to listen to the news to know the truth of that. But the Gospel goes on - "But as many as received him, to them gave he power to become the sons of God".

For all the inhumanity around us, let us be grateful for those who have received him and who go about quietly doing their work and His will without thought of reward or recognition.

They know that there is an eternal truth of much greater significance than our own triumphs and tragedies, and it is embodied by the Child in the Manger. That is their message of hope.

We can all try to reflect that message of hope in our own lives, in our actions and in our prayers. If we do, the reflection may light the way for others and help them to read the message too.
...

I am reminded this year of some lines from a Christmas hymn which many of you will know: "Yet in thy dark streets shineth the everlasting light. The hopes and fears of all the years are met in thee tonight." (1993)

Christmas tree lights remind us that light shines in the darkness.

At this time of year, few sights evoke more feelings of cheer and goodwill than the twinkling lights of a Christmas tree.

The popularity of a tree at Christmas is due in part to my great-great grandparents, Queen Victoria and Prince Albert. After this touching picture was published, many families wanted a Christmas tree of their own, and the custom soon spread. ...

It is true that the world has had to confront moments of darkness this year, but the Gospel of John contains a verse of great hope, often read at Christmas carol services: "The light shines in the darkness, and the darkness has not overcome it".

One cause for thankfulness this summer was marking 70 years since the end of the Second World War. ...

At the end of that war, the people of Oslo began sending an annual gift of a Christmas tree for Trafalgar Square.

It has 500 light bulbs and is enjoyed not just by Christians but by people of all faiths, and of none. At the very top sits a bright star, to represent the Star of Bethlehem.

The custom of topping a tree also goes back to Prince Albert's time. For his family's tree, he chose an angel, helping to remind us that the focus of the Christmas story is on one particular family.

For Joseph and Mary, the circumstances of Jesus's birth - in a stable - were far from ideal, but worse was to come as the family was forced to flee the country.

It's no surprise that such a human story still captures our imagination and continues to inspire all of us who are Christians, the world over.

Despite being displaced and persecuted throughout his short life, Christ's unchanging message was not one of revenge or violence but simply that we should love one another.

Although it is not an easy message to follow, we shouldn't be discouraged; rather, it inspires us to try harder: to be thankful for the people who bring love and happiness into our own lives, and to look for ways of spreading that love to others, whenever and wherever we can. (2015)

The Queen's historic Easter message of 2020 included these reflections.

As darkness falls on the Saturday before Easter Day, many Christians would normally light candles together. In church, one light would pass to another, spreading slowly and then more rapidly as more candles are lit. It's a way of showing how the good news of Christ's resurrection has been passed on from the first Easter by every generation until now.

This year, Easter will be different for many of us, but by keeping apart we keep others safe. But Easter isn't cancelled; indeed, we need Easter as much as ever. The discovery of the risen Christ on the first Easter Day gave his followers new hope and fresh purpose, and we can all take heart from this. We know that Coronavirus will not overcome us. As dark as death can be — particularly for those suffering with grief — light and life are greater. May the living flame of the Easter hope be a steady guide as we face the future.

I wish everyone of all faiths and denominations a blessed Easter. (2020)

The Queen's Christmas message of 2020 also focused on light.

Every year, we herald the coming of Christmas by turning on the lights. And light does more than create a festive mood. Light brings hope.

For Christians Jesus is "the light of the world" but we can't celebrate his birth today in quite the usual way. ...

This year, we celebrated International Nurses' Day on the 200th anniversary of the birth of Florence Nightingale. As with other nursing pioneers like Mary Seacole, Florence Nightingale shone a lamp of hope across the world. Today, our front-line services still shine that lamp for us, supported by the amazing achievements of modern science, and we owe them a debt of gratitude.

We continue to be inspired by the kindness of strangers, and draw comfort that even on the darkest nights, there is hope in the new dawn.

Jesus touched on this with the parable of the Good Samaritan. The man who is robbed and left at the roadside is saved by someone who did not share his religion or culture.

This wonderful story of kindness is still as relevant today. Good Samaritans have emerged across society, showing care and respect for all, regardless of gender, race, and background, reminding us that each one of us is special and equal in the eyes of God.

The teachings of Christ have served as my inner light, as has the sense of purpose we can find in coming together to worship. ...

Let the light of Christmas, the spirit of selflessness, love, and above all hope, guide us in the times ahead. It is in that spirit I wish you a very happy Christmas. (2020)

Her Majesty Queen Elizabeth II 2020

5 Love & Kindness

Love and kindness flood through the life of Jesus Christ, demonstrated most powerfully in his death and resurrection. He showed unconditional love and acceptance for all people.

Some critical religious leaders and scholars savagely criticized Jesus for his love and kindness to everyone including prostitutes, a woman accused of adultery, traitors like tax collectors who worked for the oppressive Romans, and even praising a Roman centurion for his strong faith. Jesus ate often in the homes of all kinds of people and was known as a friend of outcasts and sinners.

He didn't allow traditional religious rules to stop him from helping people in need, including healing many people at any time, even on sacred Sabbath days and in places of worship. That drew strong criticism from many religious leaders, making many of them so furious that they wanted him killed.

His love for all people and his acceptance and forgiveness amazed even his followers and many others. He told stories of how those who are forgiven much love much, and those forgiven the most often love the most.

Many writers discuss the popular five love languages – affirmation, service, gifts, time and touch. We use all these and receive them in different ways. Jesus constantly demonstrated these love languages in many ways.

He affirmed and admired faith, especially faith in him. He served daily and showed it dramatically by washing his disciples' feet the night before he died. He gave food when needed and ultimately gives eternal life to all believers. His three years of quality time with his followers prepared them to serve. His touch brought physical and spiritual healing and wholeness to many.

Most of all Jesus demonstrated his vast love in his death on our behalf. As an old hymn says, 'There was no other good enough to pay the price of sin. He only could unlock the gate of heaven and let us in."

The Queen often referred to the love and kindness seen in Jesus Christ, including these statements.

Christ taught love and charity and that we should show humanity and compassion at all times and in all situations. (1973)

I recall, especially, a dazzling spring day in Norwich when I attended the Maundy Service, the Cathedral providing a spectacular setting.

The lovely service is always a reminder of Christ's words to his disciples: "Love one another; as I have loved you". It sounds so simple yet it proves so hard to obey. ...

If only we can live up to the example of the child who was born at Christmas with a love that came to embrace the whole world. (1996)

No one is beyond the reach of God's love.

For Christians, as for all people of faith, reflection, meditation and prayer help us to renew ourselves in God's love, as we strive daily to become better people. The Christmas message shows us that this love is for everyone. There is no one beyond its reach. (2013)

Quotations about Love and Kindness

Royal Mail Castle Stamps, 1955

The Christmas message to each of us is indivisible; there can be no "Peace on earth" without "Goodwill toward men". Scientists talk of 'chain reaction' - of power releasing yet more power. This principle must be most true when it is applied to the greatest power of all: the power of love. (1955)

The power of love includes the healing power of tolerance and comradeship.

Particularly on this day of the family festival let us remember those who - like the Holy Family before them - have been driven from their homes by war or violence. We call them 'refugees': let us give them a true refuge: let us see that for them and their children there is room at the Inn. ...

The Queen said that *the healing power of tolerance, comradeship and love must be allowed to play its part. ...*

That each one of us should give this power a chance to do its work is my heartfelt message to you all upon this Christmas

Day. I can think of no better resolve to make, nor any better day on which to make it. Let us remember this during our festivities, for it is part of the Christmas message - "Goodwill toward men". (1956)

Royal Visit to Nigeria (1956)

The power of love flowers into humanity, compassion and mutual respect.

I believe that Christmas should remind us that the qualities of the human spirit are more important than material gain. Christ taught love and charity and that we should show humanity and compassion at all times and in all situations.

A lack of humanity and compassion can be very destructive - how easily this causes diversions within nations and between nations. We should remember instead how much we have in common and resolve to give expression to the best of our human qualities, not only at Christmas, but right through the year. (1973)

Jesus Christ emphasized love for all people and demonstrated it.

Christ attached supreme importance to the individual and he amazed the world in which he lived by making it clear that the unfortunate and the underprivileged had an equal place in the Kingdom of Heaven with the rich and powerful. But he also taught that man must do his best to live in harmony with man and to love his neighbours. (1982)

In 1989 The Queen read part of her Christmas speech from a podium on the stage at the Royal Albert Hall, recorded at a special Save the Children Fund charity carol concert with 2,000 attending. For the first time, an audience heard the speech prior to its international broadcast. Her unexpected speech at the event surprised everyone. She also spoke to children at the end of the broadcast. Her message urged children to preserve and protect their world:

Earth from space, NASA

The surprise Christmas Speech to the children at the charity carol concert encouraged them to be thoughtful and kind.

You've all seen pictures of the earth taken from space. Unlike all the other planets in the solar system, earth shimmers green and blue in the sunlight and looks a very pleasant place to live.

The Queen said that *technical skills are not enough by themselves. They can only come to the rescue of the planet if we also learn to live by the golden rule which Jesus Christ taught us - "love thy neighbour as thyself".*

Many of you will have heard the story of the Good Samaritan, and of how Christ answered the question (from a clever lawyer who was trying to catch him out) "Who is my neighbour?"

Jesus told of the traveller who was mugged and left injured on the roadside where several important people saw him, and passed by without stopping to help.

His neighbour was the man who did stop, cared for him, and made sure he was being well looked after before he resumed his own journey. ...

You children have something to give us which is priceless. You can still look at the world with a sense of wonder and remind us grown-ups that life is wonderful and precious. Often a child's helplessness and vulnerability bring out the best in us.

Part of that 'best in us' could be a particular tenderness towards this earth which we share as human beings, all of us, and, together, as the nations of the world, will leave to our children and our children's children. We must be kind to it for their sake.

In the hope that we will be kind and loving to one another, not just on Christmas Day, but throughout the year, I wish you all a very Happy Christmas. God bless you. (1989)

Loving one another is central in Christ's teaching and example.

Christmas is the celebration of the birth of the founder of the Christian faith, an event which took place almost 2000 years ago; every year, at this time, we are asked to look back at that extraordinary story and remind ourselves of the message which inspired Christ's followers then, and which is just as relevant today.

At Christmas I enjoy looking back on some of the events of the year. Many have their roots in history but still have a real point for us today. I recall, especially, a dazzling spring day in Norwich when I attended the Maundy Service, the Cathedral providing a spectacular setting.

The lovely service is always a reminder of Christ's words to his disciples: "Love one another; as I have loved you". It sounds so simple yet it proves so hard to obey. ...

If only we can live up to the example of the child who was born at Christmas with a love that came to embrace the whole world. If only we can let him recapture for us that time when we faced the future with childhood's unbounded faith.

Armed with that faith, the New Year, with all its challenges and chances, should hold no terrors for us, and we should be able to embark upon it undaunted. (1996)

For most of us this is a happy family day. But I am well aware that there are many of you who are alone, bereaved, or suffering. My heart goes out to you, and I pray that we, the more fortunate ones, can unite to lend a helping hand whenever it is needed, and not 'pass by on the other side'.

St Paul spoke of the first Christmas as the kindness of God dawning upon the world. The world needs that kindness now more than ever - the kindness and consideration for others that disarms malice and allows us to get on with one another with respect and affection.

Christmas reassures us that God is with us today. But, as I have discovered afresh for myself this year, he is always present in the kindness shown by our neighbours and the love of our friends and family. (1997)

6 Truth & Courage

Truth and courage characterized Jesus Christ's life and teaching. He confronted and challenged hypocrisy and evil, declaring that he is "the way, the truth, and the life." His courage led him to his brutal death on a cross and his ultimate triumph over death.

Jesus himself is the embodiment of truth and courage. He did not flinch from confronting widespread hypocrisy and hidden thoughts and desires for evil. He famously said, "You shall know the truth and the truth will set you free." Referring to himself, he went on to say, "If the Son makes you free you will be free indeed" (John 8:32, 36)

One of his famous followers, who left a life of indulgence and became a renowned advocate for truth, St Augustine of Hippo, wrote, "The truth is like a lion; you don't have to defend it. Let it loose; it will defend itself."

Clive Staples Lewis, a great writers of the twentieth century, argued in his famous 'trilemma' that Jesus is not just a great moral teacher, but for him to say what he said and do what he did he must be either a liar, a lunatic or Lord.

C S Lewis is included at Poets' Corner in Westminster Abbey. The memorial floor stone inscription has a quote from Lewis' book *The Weight of Glory*: "I believe in Christianity as I believe that the Sun has risen, not only because I see it but because by it I see everything else."

Alfred Lord Tennyson's clarion call in his poem In Memorium (Ring out, wild bells) bids farewell to the old year and welcomes the new – ring out the false, ring in the true:

Ring out the old, ring in the new,
Ring, happy bells, across the snow:

The year is going, let him go;
Ring out the false, ring in the true.

The Queen quoted from this poem and other writings in noting the value and importance of truth and courage, as in these selections.

I wonder whether you remember, during the Thanksgiving Service in St. Paul's, the congregation singing that wonderful hymn "Immortal, Invisible, God only wise".

"Now give us we pray thee the Spirit of love,
The gift of true wisdom that comes from above,
The spirit of service that has naught of pride,
The gift of true courage, and thee as our guide." ...

We know that the world can never be free from conflict and pain, but Christmas also draws our attention to all that is hopeful and good in this changing world; it speaks of values and qualities that are true and permanent and it reminds us that the world we would like to see can only come from the goodness of the heart.

When you hear the bells ringing at Christmas, think of the lines written by Tennyson:

"Ring out false pride in place and blood,
The civic slander and the spite;
Ring in the love of truth and right,
Ring in the common love of good. (1980)

And from John Bunyan's Pilgrims Progress the words of Mr Valiant for Truth:

My sword I give to him that shall succeed me in my pilgrimage and my courage and skill to him that can get it. (1957)

91

Quotations about Truth and Courage

The first televised Royal Christmas Message, 1957

Twenty-five years ago my grandfather broadcast the first of these Christmas messages. Today is another landmark because television has made it possible for many of you to see me in your homes on Christmas Day. ...

I would like to read you a few lines from 'Pilgrim's Progress', because I am sure we can say with Mr Valiant for Truth, these words:

"Though with great difficulty I am got hither, yet now I do not repent me of all the trouble I have been at to arrive where I am. My sword I give to him that shall succeed me in my pilgrimage and my courage and skill to him that can get it. My marks and scars I carry with me, to be a witness for me that I have fought his battles who now will be my rewarder." (1957)

The theme of truth and right continued in other messages.

The Queen began her message in 1980 with these words:

I was glad that the celebrations of my mother's 80th birthday last summer gave so much pleasure. I wonder whether you remember, during the Thanksgiving Service in St. Paul's, the congregation singing that wonderful hymn "Immortal, Invisible, God only wise".

"Now give us we pray thee the Spirit of love,
The gift of true wisdom that comes from above,
The spirit of service that has naught of pride,
The gift of true courage, and thee as our guide."

This Christmas Speech concluded with these words:

When you hear the bells ringing at Christmas, think of the lines written by Tennyson:

"Ring out false pride in place and blood,
The civic slander and the spite;
Ring in the love of truth and right,
Ring in the common love of good ...

Ring in the valiant man and free,
The larger heart, the kindlier hand,
Ring out the darkness of the land,
Ring in the Christ that is to be."
(1980)

7 Peace & Goodwill

Peace and goodwill toward all on earth were announced by angels at Jesus' birth. Our broken world needs that. Jesus gave his peace and on the eve of his execution he promised his peace even amid opposition and difficulties.

Peace and goodwill were announced by angels to shepherds at the time of Jesus' birth:

> Then the angel said to them, "Do not be afraid, for behold, I bring you good tidings of great joy which will be to all people. For there is born to you this day in the city of David a Saviour, who is Christ the Lord. And this *will be* the sign to you: You will find a Babe wrapped in swaddling cloths, lying in a manger."
>
> And suddenly there was with the angel a multitude of the heavenly host praising God and saying:
>
> "Glory to God in the highest,
> And on earth peace, goodwill toward men!"

That angelic declaration has resounded and echoed through the centuries and around the world as the Christmas hymn 'While shepherds watched their flocks by night' which concludes with the angels' praise:

> All glory be to God on high,
> And to the Earth be peace;
> Goodwill henceforth from heaven to men
> Begin and never cease!

Jesus Christ's birth announces peace and goodwill to all.

The famous prayer poem, attributed to St. Francis of Assisi (1182-1226), asks to be an instrument of the Lord's peace:

Lord make me an instrument of your peace
Where there is hatred let me sow love
Where there is injury, pardon
Where there is doubt, faith
Where there is despair, hope
Where there is darkness, light
And where there is sadness, joy.

O divine master grant that I may
not so much seek to be consoled as to console
to be understood as to understand
to be loved as to love.
For it is in giving that we receive
it is in pardoning that we are pardoned
And it's in dying that we are born to eternal life.
Amen

The young Queen in her first Christmas broadcast in 1952 declared that "Peace on earth, Goodwill toward men" is the eternal message of Christmas, and the desire of us all. Her Majesty's broadcasts often reminded us of this key theme of Christmas, such as these:

The message of Christmas remains the same; but humanity can only progress if we are all truly ambitious for what is good and honourable. We know the reward is peace on earth, goodwill toward men, but we cannot win it without determination and concerted effort. (1963)

At Christmas we are also reminded that it is the time of peace on earth and goodwill towards men. Yet we are all only too well aware of the tragic fighting, hatred and ill-will in so many parts of the world. (1966)

Christmas is the festival of peace. It is God's will that it should be our constant endeavour to establish 'Peace on earth, goodwill towards men'. (1968)

Quotations about Peace and Goodwill

The first Royal Christmas Message televised in colour (1967)

Modern communications make it possible for me to talk to you in your homes and to wish you a merry Christmas and a very happy New Year. These techniques of radio and television are modern, but the Christmas message is timeless.

You may have heard it very often but in the end, no matter what scientific progress we make, the message will count for nothing unless we can achieve real peace and encourage genuine goodwill between individual people and the nations of the world.

Every Christmas I am sustained and encouraged by the happiness and sense of unity which comes from seeing all the members of my family together.

I hope and pray that, with God's help, this Christmas spirit of family unity will spread and grow among our Commonwealth family of nations. (1967)

Peace and goodwill remain the great themes of Christmas.

Many ideas are being questioned today, but these great truths will continue to shine out as the light of hope in the darkness of intolerance and inhumanity. ...

Christmas is the festival of peace. It is God's will that it should be our constant endeavour to establish 'Peace on earth, goodwill towards men'. (1968)

Christmas is above all a time of new life. A time to look hopefully ahead to a future when the problems which face the world today will be seen in their true perspective.

I leave with you the old message, "On earth peace; goodwill toward men". No one has ever offered a better formula and I hope that its simple truth may yet take hold of the imagination of all mankind. (1972)

Peace and goodwill are fostered by communicating as friends.

I hope that Christmas will remind us all that it is not how we communicate but what we communicate with each other that really matters.

We in the Commonwealth are fortunate enough to belong to a world wide comradeship. Let us make the most of it; let us all resolve to communicate as friends in tolerance and understanding. Only then can we make the message of the angels come true: 'Peace on earth, goodwill towards men'. (1983)

The birth and life of the Prince of Peace is a constant theme in the broadcasts.

It is particularly at Christmas, which marks the birth of the Prince of Peace, that we should work to heal old wounds and to abandon prejudice and suspicion.

What better way of making a start than by remembering what Christ said - "Except ye become as little children, ye shall not enter into the Kingdom of Heaven". (1984)

The Queen, The Queen Mother, and Princess Margaret
50th Anniversary, end of World War II, 1995

In 1995 The Queen led national celebrations for the 50th anniversary of the end of World War II. The Christmas Broadcast reflected on the role of ordinary men and women in bringing peace to troubled places.

It is the ordinary men and women who, so often, have done more than anyone else to bring peace to troubled lands. ...

I have of course used the Christmas story before in this context. But I cannot think of any Christmas of my reign when the message of the angels has been more apt.

Think, for instance, of all the children round the world suffering from the effects of war and the unscrupulous use of power. Some of them are growing up in countries of the Commonwealth, an organisation which is proud of its devotion to the principle of good government. ...

"Blessed be the peacemakers," Christ said, "for they shall be called the children of God." It is especially to those of you, often peacemakers without knowing it, who are fearful of a troubled and uncertain future, that I bid a Happy Christmas. (1995)

Christmas is a shared festival of peace, tolerance and goodwill.

I have lived long enough to know that things never remain quite the same for very long. One of the things that has not changed all that much for me is the celebration of Christmas. It remains a time when I try to put aside the anxieties of the moment and remember that Christ was born to bring peace and tolerance to a troubled world.

The birth of Jesus naturally turns our thoughts to all new-born children and what the future holds for them. The birth of a baby brings great happiness - but then the business of growing up begins. It is a process that starts within the protection and care of parents and other members of the family - including the older generation. As with any team, there is strength in combination: what grandparent has not wished for the best possible upbringing for their grandchildren or felt an enormous sense of pride at their achievements? ...

For Christians, Christmas marks the birth of our Saviour, but it is also a wonderful occasion to bring the generations together in a shared festival of peace, tolerance and goodwill.
(2006)

The message of peace on earth and goodwill toward all is never out of date.

And suddenly there was with the angel a multitude of the heavenly host praising God and saying:

"Glory to God in the highest,
And on earth peace, goodwill[e] toward men!"
(Luke 23:13-14)

The Christmas story retains its appeal since it doesn't provide theoretical explanations for the puzzles of life. Instead, it's about the birth of a child, and the hope that birth 2,000 years ago brought to the world.

Only a few people acknowledged Jesus when he was born; now billions follow him. I believe his message of peace on earth and goodwill to all is never out of date. It can be heeded by everyone. It's needed as much as ever. (2018)

8 Compassion & Care

Compassion and care fill the story of Jesus and those who follow him faithfully. His compassion for the outcast, the sick, the despised, and the weak is legendary. He cared, and his actions demonstrated his compassion and care.

He told the famous story of the Good Samaritan who showed compassion in caring for the robbed and wounded traveller and challenged his listeners to go and to the same.

Jesus continually demonstrated love and compassion each day in his ministry and service. He was moved with compassion continually and constantly met the needs of people around him as in his acts of healing.

Many of Jesus' well known statements are about loving compassion and care, such as these:

> Love one another as I have loved you.

> By this shall everyone know that you are my disciples if you have love for one another.

> Blessed are the merciful for they shall obtain mercy.

> I say to you, love your enemies, bless those who curse you, do good to those who hate you, and pray for those who spitefully use you and persecute you, that you may be children of your Father in heaven; for He makes His sun rise on the evil and on the good, and sends rain on the just and on the unjust.

His true followers live lives of compassion and care like their leader, as do good people the world over. Many of our well known institutions for helping people were founded by Christians caring for others in orphanages, hospices, hospitals, soup kitchens, homes for the aged and shelters for people in need.

Through the years, those helping institutions, which often began with concerned individuals taking action to help others, have grown into large service providers run by churches, community groups, and government agencies. People of good will of all faiths, and of none, show this compassion and care.

Queen Elizabeth II and her family are constantly involved in supporting and encouraging people involved in caring services, meeting a vast range of needs in the community. The Queen often referred to these acts of service in her broadcasts, as in these excerpts.

That, very simply, is the message of Christmas - learning to be concerned about one another; to treat your neighbour as you would like him to treat you; and to care about the future of all life on earth. (1970)

You may be asking what can we do personally to make things better?

I believe the Christmas message provides the best clue. Goodwill is better than resentment, tolerance is better than revenge, compassion is better than anger, above all a lively concern for the interests of others as well as our own. (1974)

This message - love thy neighbour as thyself - may be for Christians 2,000 years old. But it is as relevant today as it ever was. I believe it gives us the guidance and the reassurance we need as we step over the threshold into the twenty-first century. (1999)

It is all too easy to 'turn a blind eye', 'to pass by on the other side', and leave it to experts and professionals. All the great religious teachings of the world press home the message that everyone has a responsibility to care for the vulnerable. (2007)

Quotations about Compassion and Care

Christmas Broadcast 1975

We are celebrating a birthday - the birthday of a child born nearly 2,000 years ago, who grew up and lived for only about 30 years.

That one person, by his example and by his revelation of the good which is in us all, has made an enormous difference to the lives of people who have come to understand his teaching. His simple message of love has been turning the world upside down ever since. He showed that what people are and what they do, does matter and does make all the difference.

He commanded us to love our neighbours as we love ourselves, but what exactly is meant by 'loving ourselves'? I believe it means trying to make the most of the abilities we have been given, it means caring for our talents.

It is a matter of making the best of ourselves, not just doing the best for ourselves. (1975)

That, very simply, is the message of Christmas - learning to be concerned about one another; to treat your neighbour as you would like him to treat you; and to care about the future of all life on earth. (1970)

You may be asking what can we do personally to make things better?

I believe the Christmas message provides the best clue. Goodwill is better than resentment, tolerance is better than revenge, compassion is better than anger, above all a lively concern for the interests of others as well as our own.

In times of doubt and anxiety the attitudes people show in their daily lives, in their homes, and in their work, are of supreme importance.

It is by acting in this spirit that every man, woman and child can help and 'make a difference'. (1974)

The Queen Mother, 85th birthday
Kingdom of Lesotho commemorative stamps 1985

Goodwill produces good news.

Christmas is a time of good news. I believe it is a time to look at the good things in life and to remember that there are a great many people trying to make the world a better place, even though their efforts may go unrecognised.

There is a lesson in this for us all and we should never forget our obligation to make our own individual contributions, however small, towards the sum of human goodness.

The story of the Good Samaritan reminds us of our duty to our neighbour. We should try to follow Christ's clear instruction at the end of that story: "Go and do thou likewise". (1985)

Listening to the choir from St. George's Chapel, Windsor, reminds me that this season of carols and Christmas trees is a time to take stock; a time to reflect on the events of the past year and to make resolutions for the new year ahead. ...

The future is not only about new gadgets, modern technology or the latest fashion, important as these may be. At the centre of our lives - today and tomorrow - must be the message of caring for others, the message at the heart of Christianity and of all the great religions.

This message - love thy neighbour as thyself - may be for Christians 2,000 years old. But it is as relevant today as it ever was. I believe it gives us the guidance and the reassurance we need as we step over the threshold into the twenty-first century. (1999)

Diamond Wedding Anniversary 2007

Now today, of course, marks the birth of Jesus Christ. Among other things, it is a reminder that it is the story of a family; but of a family in very distressed circumstances. Mary and Joseph found no room at the inn; they had to make do in a stable, and the new-born Jesus had to be laid in a manger. This was a family which had been shut out.

Perhaps it was because of this early experience that, throughout his ministry, Jesus of Nazareth reached out and made friends with people whom others ignored or despised. It was in this way that he proclaimed his belief that, in the end, we are all brothers and sisters in one human family.

The Christmas story also draws attention to all those people who are on the edge of society - people who feel cut off and disadvantaged; people who, for one reason or another, are not able to enjoy the full benefits of living in a civilised and law-abiding community. For these people the modern world can seem a distant and hostile place.

It is all too easy to 'turn a blind eye', 'to pass by on the other side', and leave it to experts and professionals. All the great religious teachings of the world press home the message that everyone has a responsibility to care for the vulnerable. (2007)

Jesus consistently demonstrated compassion and care.

At Christmas, we feel very fortunate to have our family around us. But for many of you, this Christmas will mean separation from loved ones and perhaps reflection on the memories of those no longer with us.

I hope that, like me, you will be comforted by the example of Jesus of Nazareth who, often in circumstances of great adversity, managed to live an outgoing, unselfish and sacrificial life. Countless millions of people around the world continue to celebrate his birthday at Christmas, inspired by his teaching. He makes it clear that genuine human happiness and satisfaction lie more in giving than receiving; more in serving than in being served.

We can surely be grateful that, two thousand years after the birth of Jesus, so many of us are able to draw inspiration from his life and message, and to find in him a source of strength and courage. I hope that the Christmas message will

encourage and sustain you too, now and in the coming year.
(2008)

Loving our neighbours involves compassion and concern.

We know that Christmas is a time for celebration and family reunions; but it is also a time to reflect on what confronts those less fortunate than ourselves, at home and throughout the world.

Christians are taught to love their neighbours, having compassion and concern, and being ready to undertake charity and voluntary work to ease the burden of deprivation and disadvantage. We may ourselves be confronted by a bewildering array of difficulties and challenges, but we must never cease to work for a better future for ourselves and for others. (2009)

9 Forgiveness & Reconciliation

Forgiveness and reconciliation flood through the life and teaching of Jesus. He did not come to judge but to love and to forgive, and he calls us to live that way also. Then we can enjoy harmony and live in reconciliation with one another.

The heart of the Christian message is about God's love and forgiveness and that we can be fully reconciled to God no matter how much we may have failed of fallen short of his goodness.

Possibly the most famous and most quoted Bible passage about God's love and forgiveness is found in the famous, immortal words of John 3:16-17 - "For God so loved the world that He gave His only begotten Son, that whoever believes in Him should not perish but have everlasting life. For God did not send His Son into the world to condemn the world, but that the world through Him might be saved."

Jesus lived a perfect life, without sin, and offered himself as the eternal sacrifice for our sin. He forgives. He reconciles us to God. We are not condemned as we trust in him.

Jesus demonstrated forgiveness as he lived among people. He often said, "Your sins are forgiven." That got into hot water with some religious people. He forgave and did not condemn a woman who committed adultery even though she was being severely condemned by others.

Forgiveness and reconciliation with God and with one another are hall marks of Christian faith and life. Jesus expected and commanded his followers to love and forgive one another and others.

Where there is injustice and where people do wrong to us it is hard to forgive and be reconciled. But when we choose to forgive then the love of God and his forgiveness can flow through us to bless others, and we also are blessed. Society changes for good when we forgive and are reconciled to one another. This is the tough and challenging Christian way of life.

The Queen also referred to the importance of forgiveness and reconciliation in her Christmas messages, as in these examples.

For me, the life of Jesus Christ, the Prince of Peace, whose birth we celebrate today, is an inspiration and an anchor in my life.

A role model of reconciliation and forgiveness, he stretched out his hands in love, acceptance and healing. Christ's example has taught me to seek to respect and value all people, of whatever faith or none. (2014)

God sent into the world a unique person - neither a philosopher nor a general, important though they are, but a Saviour, with the power to forgive. Forgiveness lies at the heart of the Christian faith. It can heal broken families, it can restore friendships and it can reconcile divided communities. It is in forgiveness that we feel the power of God's love.

Quotations about Forgiveness and Reconciliation

'Reconciliation' by Josefina de Vasconcellos at Coventry Cathedral

In the ruins of the old Coventry Cathedral is a sculpture of a man and a woman reaching out to embrace each other ... inspired by the story of a woman who crossed Europe on foot after the war to find her husband.

In 1914, many people thought the war would be over by Christmas, but sadly by then the trenches were dug and the future shape of the war in Europe was set.

But, as we know, something remarkable did happen that Christmas, exactly a hundred years ago today.

Without any instruction or command, the shooting stopped and German and British soldiers met in No Man's Land. Photographs were taken and gifts exchanged. It was a Christmas truce. ...

For me, the life of Jesus Christ, the Prince of Peace, whose birth we celebrate today, is an inspiration and an anchor in my life.

A role model of reconciliation and forgiveness, he stretched out his hands in love, acceptance and healing. Christ's example has taught me to seek to respect and value all people, of whatever faith or none.

Sometimes it seems that reconciliation stands little chance in the face of war and discord. But, as the Christmas truce a century ago reminds us, peace and goodwill have lasting power in the hearts of men and women.

On that chilly Christmas Eve in 1914 many of the German forces sang Silent Night, its haunting melody inching across the line.

That carol is still much-loved today, a legacy of the Christmas truce, and a reminder to us all that even in the unlikeliest of places hope can still be found. (2014)

Reconciliation overcomes our differences.

The Queen, President Gerald Ford, and Prince Philip
The United States of America Bicentennial 1976

Christmas is a time for reconciliation. A time not only for families and friends to come together but also for differences to be forgotten. ...

Reconciliation, like the one that followed the American War of Independence, is the product of reason, tolerance and love, and I think that Christmas is a good time to reflect on it. ...

The gift I would most value next year is that reconciliation should be found wherever it is needed. A reconciliation which would bring peace and security to families and neighbours at present suffering and torn apart.

Remember that good spreads outwards and every little does help. Mighty things from small beginnings grow as indeed they grew from the small child of Bethlehem. ...

I wish you all a very happy Christmas and may the New Year bring reconciliation between all people. (1976)

The Silver Jubilee celebrated 25 years of The Queen's reign in 1977.

Last Christmas I said that my wish for 1977 was that it should be a year of reconciliation. You have shown by the way in which you have celebrated the Jubilee that this was not an impossible dream. Thank you all for your response. ...

The Jubilee celebrations in London started with a Service of Thanksgiving in St. Paul's Cathedral. To me this was a thanksgiving for all the good things for which our Commonwealth stands - the comradeship and co-operation it inspires and the friendship and tolerance it encourages. These are the qualities needed by all mankind.

The evening before the Service I lit one small flame at Windsor and a chain of bonfires spread throughout Britain and on across the world to New Zealand and Australia.

My hope this Christmas is that the Christian spirit of reconciliation may burn as strongly in our hearts during the coming year. (1977)

Reconciliation and forgiveness lie at the heart of the Christian faith.

Finding hope in adversity is one of the themes of Christmas. Jesus was born into a world full of fear. The angels came to frightened shepherds with hope in their voices: 'Fear not', they urged, 'we bring you tidings of great joy, which shall be to all people. For unto you is born this day in the City of David a Saviour who is Christ the Lord.'

Although we are capable of great acts of kindness, history teaches us that we sometimes need saving from ourselves - from our recklessness or our greed.

God sent into the world a unique person - neither a philosopher nor a general, important though they are, but a Saviour, with the power to forgive. Forgiveness lies at the heart of the Christian faith. It can heal broken families, it can restore friendships and it can reconcile divided communities. It is in forgiveness that we feel the power of God's love.

In the last verse of this beautiful carol, O Little Town of Bethlehem, there's a prayer:
O Holy Child of Bethlehem,
Descend to us we pray.
Cast out our sin
And enter in.
Be born in us today.

It is my prayer that on this Christmas day we might all find room in our lives for the message of the angels and for the love of God through Christ our Lord. (2011)

Jesus Christ's generous love and example inspire us.

Today, we celebrate Christmas, which, itself, is sometimes described as a festival of the home. Families travel long distances to be together.

Volunteers and charities, as well as many churches, arrange meals for the homeless and those who would otherwise be alone on Christmas Day. We remember the birth of Jesus Christ, whose only sanctuary was a stable in Bethlehem. He knew rejection, hardship and persecution.

And, yet, it is Jesus Christ's generous love and example which has inspired me through good times and bad. Whatever your own experience is this year, wherever and however you are watching, I wish you a peaceful and very happy Christmas. (2017)

10 Respect & Tolerance

Respect and tolerance can be found in living together in the harmony of mutual acceptance. We all differ, but our differences can enrich our lives and our understanding of one another. Jesus Christ mixed freely with all kinds of people in all levels of society and demonstrated acceptance, forgiveness, and love.

Jesus held strong convictions about truth and righteousness and yet he showed outstanding acceptance of all kinds of people including those who differed in their lifestyle from his own. He freely forgave and challenged his followers to love one another and also to love their enemies.

We can honour one another with the tolerance of humble conviction that also acknowledges and respects our differences. We have much to learn from one another and in many ways we can help and encourage each other.

Unfortunately history is littered with sectarian and cultural conflicts where hate replaced love and respect. If we can hear and heed the teaching and example of the Prince of Peace we can live together in respect and tolerance while humbly holding our own convictions.

Throughout Her Majesty's long reign and in over 70 personal broadcasts The Queen has emphasized the values of mutual respect and tolerance, as in these statements.

I am afraid that the Christmas message of goodwill has usually evaporated by the time Boxing Day is over. This year I hope we will continue to remember the many innocent victims of violence and intolerance and the suffering of their families. Christians are taught to love their neighbours, not just at Christmas, but all the year round. (1987)

This Christmas we can take heart in seeing how, in the former Soviet Union and Eastern Europe, where it has endured years of persecution and hardship, the Christian faith is once again thriving and able to spread its message of unselfishness, compassion and tolerance. (1991)

This Christmas, as we pray for peace at home and abroad - not least in Russia itself - we can also give thanks that such cathedrals and churches will be full and that the great bells, which greeted us, will be ringing out to celebrate our Saviour's birth.

Christ taught us to love our enemies and to do good to them that hate us. It is a hard lesson to learn, but this year we have seen shining examples of that generosity of spirit which alone can banish division and prejudice.

... If we resolve to be considerate and to help our neighbours; to make friends with people of different races and religions; and, as our Lord said, to look to our own faults before we criticise others, we will be keeping faith with those who landed in Normandy and fought so doggedly for their belief in freedom, peace and human decency. (1994)

Religion and culture are much in the news these days, usually as sources of difference and conflict, rather than for bringing people together. But the irony is that every religion has something to say about tolerance and respecting others. (2004)

Quotations about Respect and Tolerance

Remembrance Day

The Queen referred to the Remembrance Day bombing in Enniskillen, Northern Ireland, in 1987 and stressed the importance of tolerance and forgiveness.

From time to time we also see some inspiring examples of tolerance. Mr Gordon Wilson, whose daughter Marie lost her life in the horrifying explosion at Enniskillen on Remembrance Sunday, impressed the whole world by the depth of his forgiveness.

His strength, and that of his wife, and the courage of their daughter, came from their Christian conviction. All of us will echo their prayer that out of the personal tragedies of Enniskillen may come a reconciliation between the communities. ...

I am afraid that the Christmas message of goodwill has usually evaporated by the time Boxing Day is over. This year I hope we will continue to remember the many innocent victims of violence and intolerance and the suffering of their families. Christians are taught to love their neighbours, not just at Christmas, but all the year round.

I hope we will all help each other to have a happy Christmas and, when the New Year comes, resolve to work for tolerance and understanding between all people. (1987)

We can resolve disputes in peace and justice.

Nowadays there are all too many causes that press their claims with a loud voice and a strong arm rather than with the language of reason. We must not allow ourselves to be too discouraged as we confront them.

Let us remember that Christ did not promise the earth to the powerful. The resolve of those who endure and resist these activities should not be underestimated. ...

I pray also that we may all be blessed with something of their spirit. Then we would find it easier to solve our disputes in peace and justice, wherever they occur, and that inheritance of the earth which Christ promised, not to the strong, but to the meek, would be that much closer. (1990)

Comments referred to changes in Eastern Europe and Russia in the 1990s.

This Christmas we can take heart in seeing how, in the former Soviet Union and Eastern Europe, where it has endured years of persecution and hardship, the Christian faith is once again thriving and able to spread its message of unselfishness, compassion and tolerance. (1991)

I never thought it would be possible in my lifetime to join with the Patriarch of Moscow and his congregation in a service in that wonderful cathedral in the heart of the Moscow Kremlin.

This Christmas, as we pray for peace at home and abroad - not least in Russia itself - we can also give thanks that such cathedrals and churches will be full and that the great bells, which greeted us, will be ringing out to celebrate our Saviour's birth. ...

Christ taught us to love our enemies and to do good to them that hate us. It is a hard lesson to learn, but this year we have seen shining examples of that generosity of spirit which alone can banish division and prejudice.

... If we resolve to be considerate and to help our neighbours; to make friends with people of different races and religions; and, as our Lord said, to look to our own faults before we criticise others, we will be keeping faith with those who landed in Normandy and fought so doggedly for their belief in freedom, peace and human decency. (1994)

Everyone is our neighbour.

Religion and culture are much in the news these days, usually as sources of difference and conflict, rather than for bringing people together. But the irony is that every religion has something to say about tolerance and respecting others.

For me as a Christian one of the most important of these teachings is contained in the parable of the Good Samaritan, when Jesus answers the question "who is my neighbour".

It is a timeless story of a victim of a mugging who was ignored by his own countrymen but helped by a foreigner - and a despised foreigner at that.

The implication drawn by Jesus is clear. Everyone is our neighbour, no matter what race, creed or colour. The need to look after a fellow human being is far more important than any cultural or religious differences. (2004)

Appendix

Poets and songsters give us hymns and carols that help us celebrate Christmas.

Many YouTube recordings of The Queen's Christmas Broadcasts include choirs and bands singing and playing Christmas Carols. A list of these is included in the next pages of this Appendix.

This Appendix includes some well-known Christmas Carols that tell the Christmas Message as found in the hymn books of most denominations. They are popular in Christmas celebrations and concerts such as Carols by Candlelight, and in churches in December.

Also included in the Appendix are some key resources related to The Queen's Christmas Broadcasts and some further information about *Renewal Journal* resources.

Most of this Appendix is reproduced here from my previous companion book *The Queen's Christmas & Easter Messages*. That book has a double page for each year of Her Majesty's long reign. The Gift Edition is also available in colour.

Carols and Songs included in
The Queen's Christmas Broadcasts

1984
The First Noel by background orchestral music

1986
Away in a Manger by carollers in the royal stable

1998
Ding Dong Merrily on High by background singers

1999
Once in Royal David's City by St George's Chapel Boys Choir

2001
O Come all ye Faithful and **Hark the Herald Angels Sing** by choristers and a cathedral congregation

2004
Surrounded by His Love by Sir John Cass's Foundation Primary School Choir

2005
Hark the Herald Angels Sing by Her Majesty's Chapel Royal Boys Choir

2006
Ding Dong Merrily on High by youth choir

2007
O Little Town of Bethlehem by children singing in the background

2010
While Shepherds Watched by Her Majesty's Chapel Royal Boys Choir with children reading from Luke, chapter 2.

2011
O Little Town of Bethlehem by the Royal Guards Band

2012
In the Bleak Midwinter by the Military Wives Choir

2013
The First Noel by the Royal Guards Band

2014
Silent Night by the Royal Band

2015
Away in a Manger by the Children of Her Majesty's Chapel Royal

2016
Gloucestershire Wassail by the Royal Guards Band

2017
It Came upon the Midnight Clear by the Commonwealth Youth Orchestra and Choir

2018
Once in Royal David's City by the Kings College Chapel Choir, Cambridge

2019

It Came upon the Midnight Clear by the Choir of St George's Chapel with Her Majesty's Tri-Service Orchestra

2020

Joy to the World by the Lewisham Greenwich National Health Service Choir.

Find these recitals by searching 'YouTube The Queen's Christmas Message' with the year, eg. YouTube The Queen's Christmas Message 2020.

The following pages of this Appendix include many of the well-known carols, songs and hymns used at Christmas celebrations and in church services. They celebrate the Christmas Message with beautiful lyrics set to inspiring music.

O Come, All Ye Faithful

Adeste fideles læti triumphantes,	O come, all ye faithful, joyful and triumphant!
Venite, venite in Bethlehem.	O come ye, O come ye to Bethlehem;
Natum videte	Come and behold him
Regem angelorum:	Born the King of Angels:
Venite adoremus (3×)	O come, let us adore Him, (3×)
Dominum.	Christ the Lord.
Deum de Deo, lumen de lumine	God of God, light of light,
Gestant puellæ viscera	Lo, he abhors not the Virgin's womb;
Deum verum, genitum non factum.	Very God, begotten, not created:
Venite adoremus (3×)	O come, let us adore Him, (3×)
Dominum.	Christ the Lord.
Cantet nunc io, chorus angelorum;	Sing, choirs of angels, sing in exultation,
Cantet nunc aula cælestium,	Sing, all ye citizens of Heaven above!
Gloria, gloria in excelsis Deo,	Glory to God, glory in the highest:
Venite adoremus (3×)	O come, let us adore Him, (3×)
Dominum.	Christ the Lord.

Ergo qui natus die hodierna. Yea, Lord, we greet thee,
born this happy morning;
Jesu, tibi sit gloria, Jesus, to thee be glory given!
Patris æterni Verbum caro factum. Word of the Father, now in
flesh appearing!
Venite adoremus (3×) O come, let us adore Him,
(3×)
Dominum. Christ the Lord

Latin: John Francis Wade, 1751
English: Frederick Oakeley, 1841
Music: Adeste Fideles, 1751

Silent Night

Stille Nacht, heilige Nacht,
Alles schläft; einsam wacht
Nur das traute hochheilige
Paar.
Holder Knabe im lockigen
Haar,
Schlaf in himmlischer Ruh!
Schlaf in himmlischer Ruh!

Stille Nacht, heilige Nacht,
Hirten erst kundgemacht
Durch der Engel Halleluja,
Tönt es laut von fern und
nah:
Christ, der Retter ist da!
Christ, der Retter ist da!

Stille Nacht, heilige Nacht,
Gottes Sohn, o wie lacht
Lieb' aus deinem göttlichen
Mund,
Da uns schlägt die rettende
Stund'.
Christ, in deiner Geburt!
Christ, in deiner Geburt!

Silent night, holy night,
All is calm, all is bright
Round yon virgin mother
and child.
Holy infant, so tender and
mild,
Sleep in heavenly peace,
Sleep in heavenly peace.

Silent night, holy night,
Shepherds quake at the
sight;
Glories stream from heaven
afar,
Heavenly hosts sing Alleluia!
Christ the Saviour is born,
Christ the Saviour is born!

Silent night, holy night,
Son of God, love's pure light;
Radiant beams from thy holy
face
With the dawn of redeeming
grace,
Jesus, Lord, at thy birth,
Jesus, Lord, at thy birth.

German: Joseph Mohr, 1818
English: John Freeman Young, 1859
Music: Franz Xaver Gruber, 1818

Angels from the Realms of Glory

Angels from the realms of Glory
Wing your flight o'er all the earth;
Ye who sang creation's story,
Now proclaim Messiah's birth:

Chorus:
Come and worship, come and worship,
Worship Christ, the newborn King.

Shepherds, in the fields abiding,
Watching o'er your flocks by night,
God with man is now residing,
Yonder shines the infant light:

Sages, leave your contemplations,
Brighter visions beam afar;
Seek the great Desire of nations,
Ye have seen his natal star:

Sinners, wrung with true repentance,
Doomed for guilt to endless pains,
Justice now revokes the sentence,
Mercy calls you—break your chains:

Though an infant now we view him,
He shall fill his Father's throne,
Gather all the nations to him;
Every knee shall then bow down:

All creation, join in praising
God the Father, Spirit, Son,
Evermore your voices raising,
To th'eternal Three in One:

Lyrics: James Montgomery, 1816
Music: "Regent Square," Henry Smart, 1816

Angels We Have Heard on High

Angels we have heard on high
Sweetly singing o'er the plain
And the mountains in reply
Echoing their joyous strains

Chorus:
Gloria, in excelsis Deo!
Gloria, in excelsis Deo!

Shepherds, why this jubilee?
Why your joyous strains prolong?
What the gladsome tidings be?
Which inspire your heavenly songs?

Come to Bethlehem and see
Christ Whose birth the angels sing;
Come, adore on bended knee,
Christ, the Lord, the newborn King.

See Him in a manger laid,
Jesus, Lord of heaven and earth;
Mary, Joseph, lend your aid,
With us sing our Savior's birth.

Gloria, in excelsis Deo!
Gloria, in excelsis Deo!

Lyrics: James Chadwick, 1862
Music: French Carol
Music: "Gloria", Edward Shippen Barnes, 1937

Away in a Manger

Away in a manger, no crib for a bed,
The little Lord Jesus laid down his sweet head.
The stars in the bright sky looked down where he lay,
The little Lord Jesus asleep on the hay.

The cattle are lowing, the baby awakes,
But little Lord Jesus, no crying he makes.
I love thee, Lord Jesus! look down from the sky,
And stay by my cradle till morning is nigh.

Be near me, Lord Jesus; I ask thee to stay
Close by me forever, and love me I pray.
Bless all the dear children in thy tender care,
And take us to heaven to live with thee there.

Lyrics: Author unknown, 1885.
Music: William J. Kirkpatrick, 1895

Christians, Awake

Christians, awake! Salute the happy morn
whereon the Saviour of the world was born;
rise to adore the mystery of love,
which hosts of angels chanted from above;
with them the joyful tidings first begun,
of God incarnate and the virgin's Son.

Then to the watchful shepherds it was told,
who heard th'angelic herald's voice, "Behold,
I bring good tidings of a Saviour's birth
to you and all the nations of the earth;
this day hath God fulfilled His promised Word;
this day is born a Saviour, Christ the Lord."

This may we hope, th'angelic hosts among,
to sing, redeemed a glad triumphal song.
He that was born upon this joyful day
around us all His glory shall display.
Saved by His love, incessantly we sing
eternal praise to heav'n's almighty King.

Lyrics: John Byrom, 1741
Music: "Yorkshire," John Wainwright, 1750

Ding dong Merrily on High

Ding dong merrily on high,
In heav'n the bells are ringing:
Ding dong! Verily the sky
Is riv'n with angel singing.
Gloria, Hosanna in excelsis!

E'en so here below, below,
Let steeple bells be swungen,
And "Io, io, io!"
By priest and people sungen.

Pray you, dutifully prime
Your matin chime, ye ringers
May you beautifully rime
Your evetime song, ye singers
Gloria, Hosanna in excelsis!
[Glory. Hosanna in the highest!]

Lyrics: George Ratcliffe Woodward, 1924
Music: **Branle** de l'Official, 1589

In the Bleak Mid-Winter

In the bleak mid-winter
Frosty wind made moan;
Earth stood hard as iron,
Water like a stone;
Snow had fallen, snow on snow,
Snow on snow,
In the bleak mid-winter
Long ago.

Our God, heaven cannot hold Him
Nor earth sustain,
Heaven and earth shall flee away
When He comes to reign:
In the bleak mid-winter
A stable-place sufficed
The Lord God Almighty —
Jesus Christ.

Enough for Him, whom Cherubim
Worship night and day,
A breastful of milk
And a mangerful of hay;
Enough for Him, whom Angels
Fall down before,
The ox and ass and camel
Which adore.

Angels and Archangels
May have gathered there,
Cherubim and seraphim
Thronged the air;
But only His Mother
In her maiden bliss
Worshipped the Beloved
With a kiss.

What can I give Him,
Poor as I am? —
If I were a Shepherd
I would bring a lamb;
If I were a Wise Man
I would do my part, —
Yet what I can I give Him, —
Give my heart.

Lyrics: Christina Rossetti, 1872
Music: "Cranham," Gustav Holst, 1906

It Came upon the Midnight Clear

It came upon the midnight clear,
That glorious song of old,
From angels bending near the earth,
To touch their harps of gold:
"Peace on the earth, goodwill to men,
From heaven's all-gracious King."
The world in solemn stillness lay,
To hear the angels sing.

Still through the cloven skies they come,
With peaceful wings unfurled,
And still their heavenly music floats
O'er all the weary world;
Above its sad and lowly plains,
They bend on hovering wing,
And ever o'er its babel sounds
The blessed angels sing.

Yet with the woes of sin and strife
The world has suffered long;
Beneath the angel-strain have rolled
Two thousand years of wrong;
And man, at war with man, hears not
The love-song which they bring;
O hush the noise, ye men of strife,
And hear the angels sing.

And ye, beneath life's crushing load,
Whose forms are bending low,
Who toil along the climbing way
With painful steps and slow,
Look now! for glad and golden hours
Come swiftly on the wing.
O rest beside the weary road,
And hear the angels sing!

For lo! the days are hastening on,
By prophet bards foretold,
When with the ever-circling years
Comes round the age of gold
When peace shall over all the earth
Its ancient splendours fling,
And the whole world give back the song
Which now the angels sing.

Lyrics: Edmund H. Sears, 1849
Music: "Carol," Richard Storrs Willis, 1850
Music: "Noel," English Melody adapted by Arthur
Sullivan, 1874

Joy to the World

Joy to the world, the Lord is come!
Let earth receive her King;
Let every heart prepare Him room,
And heav'n and nature sing,
And heav'n and nature sing,
And heav'n, and heav'n, and nature sing.

Joy to the earth, the Saviour reigns!
Let men their songs employ;
While fields and floods, rocks, hills, and plains
Repeat the sounding joy,
Repeat the sounding joy,
Repeat, repeat, the sounding joy.

No more let sins and sorrows grow,
Nor thorns infest the ground;
He comes to make His blessings flow
Far as the curse is found,
Far as the curse is found,
Far as, far as, the curse is found.

He rules the world with truth and grace,
And makes the nations prove
The glories of His righteousness,
And wonders of His love,
And wonders of His love,
And wonders, wonders, of His love.

Lyrics: Isaac Watts, 1719
Music: "Antioch" arranged from George Friedrich
Handel, 1833

O Little Town of Bethlehem

O little town of Bethlehem
How still we see thee lie!
Above thy deep and dreamless sleep
   The silent stars go by.
Yet in thy dark streets shineth
   The everlasting Light;
The hopes and fears of all the years
   Are met in thee to-night.

O morning stars, together
   Proclaim the holy birth!
And praises sing to God the King,
   And peace to men on earth.
For Christ is born of Mary
   And gathered all above,
While mortals sleep the Angels keep
   Their watch of wondering love.

How silently, how silently,
   The wondrous gift is given;
So God imparts to human hearts
   The blessings of His Heaven.
No ear may hear His coming,
   But in this world of sin,
Where meek souls will receive Him still,
   The dear Christ enters in.

O holy Child of Bethlehem,
   Descend to us, we pray!
Cast out our sin and enter in,
   Be born in us to-day.
We hear the Christmas angels,
   The great glad tidings tell;
O come to us, abide with us,
   Our Lord Emmanuel!

Lyrics: Phillips Brooks, 1868
Music: "St. Louis," Lewis Henry Redner, 1868

Once in Royal David's City

Once in royal David's city
Stood a lowly cattle shed,
Where a mother laid her Baby
In a manger for His bed:
Mary was that mother mild,
Jesus Christ her little Child.

He came down to earth from heaven,
Who is God and Lord of all,
And His shelter was a stable,
And His cradle was a stall;
With the poor, and mean, and lowly,
Lived on earth our Saviour holy.

And through all His wondrous childhood
He would honour and obey,
Love and watch the lowly maiden,
In whose gentle arms He lay:
Christian children all must be
Mild, obedient, good as He.

For he is our childhood's pattern;
Day by day, like us He grew;
He was little, weak and helpless,
Tears and smiles like us He knew;
And He feeleth for our sadness,
And He shareth in our gladness.

And our eyes at last shall see Him,
Through His own redeeming love;
For that Child so dear and gentle
Is our Lord in heaven above,
And He leads His children on
To the place where He is gone.

Not in that poor lowly stable,
With the oxen standing by,
We shall see Him; but in heaven,
Set at God's right hand on high;
Where like stars His children crowned
All in white shall wait around.

Lyrics: Cecil Frances Humphreys Alexander, 1848
Music: "Irby," Henry John Gauntlett, 1849

Surrounded by His Love

The Lord is my shepherd
He'll watch over me
Whatever I go through
He's all that I need
Wherever he leads me
I know sure enough
I will live my life
Surrounded by his love

The Lord is my shepherd
He'll stay by my side
When I feel afraid
In the darkest of nights
I'm safe in the hands
Of the Father above
I will live my life
Surrounded by his love

And I will sing his praise

Surely goodness and mercy are following me
All of the days of my life
Now and forever my home will be
Here in the house of the Lord
Surrounded by his love

The Lord is my shepherd
He's gentle and strong
I know in his presence
I'll always belong
The peace that he gives me
Is more than enough
I will live my life
Surrounded by his love

Lyrics: Paul Field, 1997
Music: Daybreak Music/Elevation, 1997

The First Noel

The First Noel the angel did say
Was to certain poor shepherds
in fields as they lay;
In fields as they lay, keeping their sheep,
On a cold winter's night that was so deep.

Chorus:
Noel, Noel, Noel, Noel,
Born is the King of Israel.

They looked up and saw a star
Shining in the east beyond them far,
And to the earth it gave great light,
And so it continued both day and night.

And by the light of that same star
Three wise men came from country far;
To seek for a king was their intent,
And to follow the star wherever it went.

This star drew nigh to the northwest,
O'er Bethlehem it took it rest,
And there it did both stop and stay
Right over the place where Jesus lay.

Then entered in those wise men three
Full reverently upon their knee,
and offered there in his presence
Their gold, and myrrh, and frankincense.

Then let us all with one accord
Sing praises to our heavenly Lord;
That hath made heaven and earth of naught,
And with his blood mankind hath bought.

Noel, Noel, Noel, Noel,
Born is the King of Israel.

Lyrics: William Sandys, Davies Gilbert, 1823
Music: John Stainer, 1871

While Shepherds Watched their Flocks

While shepherds watched their flocks by night,
All seated on the ground,
The angel of the Lord came down,
And glory shone around.

"Fear not!" said he, for mighty dread
Had seized their troubled mind;
"Glad tidings of great joy I bring
To you and all mankind.

"To you, in David's town, this day
Is born of David's line
A Saviour, who is Christ the Lord,
And this shall be the sign:

"The heav'nly Babe you there shall find
To human view displayed,
All meanly wrapped in swathing bands,
And in a manger laid."

Thus spake the seraph and forthwith
Appeared a shining throng
Of angels praising God on high,
Who thus addressed their song:

"All glory be to God on high,
And to the Earth be peace;
Good will henceforth from heav'n to men
Begin and never cease!"

Lyrics: Nathan Tate, 1700
Music: George Friedrich Handel, 1728

Messiah - Selections

Messiah is an English-language oratorio composed in 1741 by George Friedrich Handel, with a scriptural text compiled by Charles Jennens from the King James Bible, and from the version of the *Psalms* included with the *Book of Common Prayer*.

In Part I the text begins with prophecies by Isaiah and others, and moves to the annunciation to the shepherds, the only "scene" taken from the Gospels.

In Part II, Handel concentrates on the Passion and ends with the "Hallelujah" chorus.

In Part III he covers the resurrection of the dead and Christ's glorification in heaven.

It is reported that when King George II attended a royal performance of *Messiah* he stood up for the *Hallelujah Chorus* in honour of the King of kings. When the king stood everyone in his presence had to stand. So it became tradition for the audience to stand up when the *Hallelujah Chorus* is sung, as millions of us have done in honour of the King of kings.

Chorus — Isaiah 9:6
For unto us a Child is born, unto us a Son is given: and the government shall be upon His shoulder: and His name shall be called Wonderful, Counsellor, the mighty God, the everlasting Father, the Prince of Peace.

Pifa (Pastoral Symphony)

Soprano Recitative — Luke 2:8-11, 13

There were shepherds abiding in the field, keeping watch over their flocks by night.

And lo! the angel of the Lord came upon them, and the glory of the Lord shone round about them: and they were sore afraid.

And the angel said unto them, Fear not; for, behold, I bring you good tidings of great joy, which shall be to all people. For unto you is born this day in the city of David a Saviour, which is Christ the Lord.

And suddenly there was with the angel a multitude of the heavenly host praising God, and saying,

Chorus — Luke 2:14

Glory to God in the highest, and peace on earth, good will toward men.

Chorus — Revelation 19:6, 11:15, 19:16

Hallelujah! for the Lord God Omnipotent reigneth.

The Kingdom of this world is become the Kingdom of our Lord, and of His Christ;

and He shall reign for ever and ever.

King of kings, and Lord of lords.

Hallelujah!

Lyrics: Holy Bible, Authorised Version, 1611, arranged by Charles Jennens, 1741
Music: George Friedrich Handel, 1741

Resources

YouTube Videos and Information

The Queen's Christmas Broadcast 2019
https://www.youtube.com/watch?v=HD5oZDKqJWs

Cue The Queen: Celebrating the Christmas Message (BBC One, YouTube)

The Royal Family, The Christmas Broadcast
https://www.royal.uk/christmas-broadcast-2017

Wikipedia, *Royal Christmas Message*.
https://en.wikipedia.org/wiki/Royal_Christmas_Message

The Royal Family: Facebook
https://www.facebook.com/TheBritishMonarchy/

The Queen's
Christmas & Easter
Messages
Queen Elizabeth II describes the
significance of Christmas & Easter

Geoffrey Waugh

The Queen's Christmas & Easter Messages

Queen Elizabeth II describes the Significance of Christmas & Easter

A double page for each year of The Queen's long reign.

Endorsements of

The Queen's Christmas & Easter Messages

1. I haven't seen anyone else draw the events of these years together in this way before. Using the Queen's speeches not only ties in the unfolding events of our time but reveals a deep spiritual glue that provides a fascinating and intimate insight into the personal life of our Queen. A fascinating read. 5 Stars. - Rev Philip Waugh (Minister)

2. *'The Christmas Message'* is an appealing, highly unusual and very creative anthology. After an introduction about the Queen's public expression of faith, Geoff Waugh provides a selection of noteworthy passages about Christmas from the Queen's Christmas messages. He sets them into context by brief historical references, photos, and Christmas stamps. Finally there is an epilogue of famous Christmas hymns and carols including those used in the Christmas Broadcasts. This book would be the perfect Christmas present. - Alison Sherrington (Author)

3. The strength of the Commonwealth of Nations is the application of Christ's teaching of peace and goodwill to all, a thread that follows through each of the broadcasts of Her

Majesty's Christmas Messages and is embodied in The Queen's own testament in these messages.

A new and innovative approach to the Christmas Story and its clear message of peace and goodwill to all. It is a rewarding experience to read it from cover to cover. - Don Hill (Consultant)

4. What an amazing collection! This has so many wonderful Christmas messages and is a great addition to any family during the holiday season. - 5 stars. Jenny & Benny (Amazon)

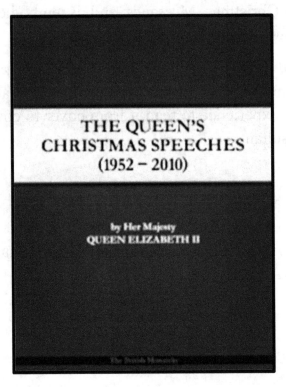

Her Majesty Queen Elizabeth II. *The Queen's Christmas Speeches*
(1952 - 2010).
The British Monarchy. Kindle Edition.

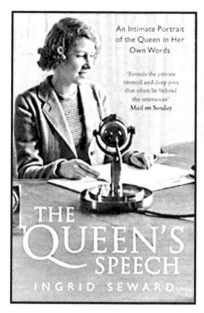

Ingrid Seward (2015), *The Queen's Speech.* Simon & Schuster.

William Shawcross (2016). *The Servant Queen and the King She Serves.*
The Bible Society.

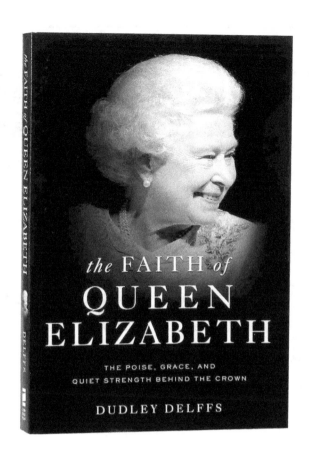

Dudley Delffs (2019), *The Faith of Queen Elizabeth.*
Zondervan.

Basic Edition in print and Gift Edition in colour

Inspiration

Short stories to touch your heart

Renewal Journal publication

www.renewaljournal.com

Basic Edition in print and Gift Edition in colour

The Lion of Judah: King of Kings and Lord of Lords

A devotional commentary on Jesus, the Lion of Judah
Six books compiled into one volume.

Introduction

1. The Titles of Jesus

2. The Reign of Jesus

3. The Life of Jesus

4. The Death of Jesus

5. The Resurrection of Jesus

6. The Spirit of Jesus

Conclusion: The Lion of Judah

Basic Edition in print and Gift Edition in colour

Discovering Aslan: High King above all Kings in Narnia

A devotional commentary on Jesus, the Lion of Judah
Seven books compiled into one volume.

Prologue & Introduction

1. The Lion, the Witch and the Wardrobe
2. Prince Caspian
3. The Voyage of the Dawn Treader
4. The Silver Chair
5. The Horse and His Boy
6. The Magician's Nephew
7. The Last Battle
Conclusion & Epilogue

Renewal Journal publication
www.renewaljournal.com

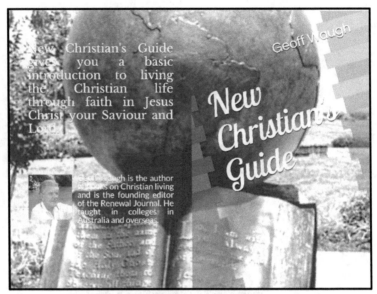

New Christian's Guide gives you a basic introduction to living the Christian life through faith in Jesus Christ your Saviour and Lord.

Geoff Waugh

New Christians Guide

Geoff Waugh is the author of books on Christian living and is the founding editor of the Renewal Journal. He taught in colleges in Australia and overseas.

Basic Edition in print and Gift Edition in colour

New Christians Guide

Introduction: Welcome to God's Family

1 Love God
Faith in God – God our Father
Follow Me – Jesus our Lord
Filled with the Spirit – Holy Spirit our Guide

2 Love Others
Love one another
Serve one another
Encourage one another

Renewal Journal publication
www.renewaljournal.com

Renewal Journal

www.renewaljournal.com

The Renewal Journal website gives links to Renewal Journals, Books, Blogs

Free subscription gives you updates for new Blogs and free offers including free PDF Books

About the Editor

The Rev Dr Geoff Waugh is the founding editor of the *Renewal Journal* and author of books on ministry and mission. He taught Anglican, Catholic and Uniting Church (formerly Congregational, Methodist and Presbyterian) students in Trinity Theological College and the School of Theology of Griffith University as well as at Christian Heritage College in Brisbane, Australia. He taught in schools and Bible Colleges in Papua New Guinea and in the South Pacific with Baptist and Churches of Christ missions and led short-term missions in Africa, Europe, South-East Asia, and in the South Pacific islands.

His books and the *Renewal Journals* are available from Amazon, Kindle and Distributors, with PDF versions available to download in colour from the **Renewal Journal** website.

Geoff and Meg have been blessed with three adult children and eight grandchildren, and have celebrated Christmas with five generations including parents and grandparents, proclaiming the Christmas Message:

Fear not: for, behold, I bring you good tidings of great joy, which shall be to all people. For unto you is born this day in the city of David a Saviour, who is Christ the Lord. (Luke 2:11)